NORTH AMERICAN
ROAD TRIPS

Unforgettable Journeys of a Lifetime

NORTH AMERICAN ROAD TRIPS

UNFORGETTABLE JOURNEYS OF A LIFETIME

MARTIN DERRICK

CHARTWELL BOOKS

Inspiring | Educating | Creating | Entertaining

Brimming with creative inspiration, how-to projects, and useful
information to enrich your everyday life, Quarto Knows is a favorite
destination for those pursuing their interests and passions. Visit our
site and dig deeper with our books into your area of interest:
Quarto Creates, Quarto Cooks, Quarto Homes, Quarto Lives,
Quarto Drives, Quarto Explores, Quarto Gifts, or Quarto Kids.

This edition published in 2018 by Chartwell Books,
an imprint of The Quarto Group
142 West 36th Street, 4th Floor
New York, NY, 10018, USA
T (212) 779-4972 F (212) 779-6058
www.QuartoKnows.com

Produced by BlueRed Press Ltd
Copyright © 2018 by BlueRed Press Ltd.

Chartwell Books titles are also available at discount for retail, wholesale, promotional, and bulk
purchase. For details, contact the Special Sales Manager by email at specialsales@quarto.com or
by mail at The Quarto Group, Attn: Special Sales Manager, 401 Second Avenue North, Suite 310,
Minneapolis, MN 55401, USA.

10 9 8 7 6 5 4 3 2

ISBN: 978-0-7858-3585-1

Text by Martin Derrick
Designed by Sunita Gahir

Printed in China

IMAGES **Page 1:** The dramatic Overseas Highway that runs the length of the Florida Keys from Miami to Key West. **Page 2-3:** At 6,646 ft (2,026 m) Logan Pass is the highest point on the Going-to-the-Sun Road. It's also one of the most popular places to stop along the route. **Page 4-5:** A misty Margaree Valley on Cape Breton Island, Nova Scotia, Canada.

CONTENTS

INTRODUCTION   6

Pali Highway, Hawaii 16
Hawaii Belt Road, Hawaii 20
Seward Highway, Alaska 26
Anchorage to Valdez, Alaska 32
Chuckanut Drive, Washington 36
Gold Rush Trail, California 40
Pacific Coast Highway I, California 44
Pacific Coast Highway II, California 48
Highway 120 Over the Sierra Nevada
   and the Tioga Pass, California 52
Columbia River Scenic Byway, Oregon 64
Las Vegas to Death Valley, Nevada 68
Going-to-the-Sun-Road, Montana 74
Utah Scenic Byway 12, Utah 78
Monument Valley, Arizona – Utah 82
San Juan Skyway
   and the Million Dollar Highway, Colorado ... 86
Pikes Peak Highway, Colorado 94
Turquoise Trail, New Mexico 100
Texas Hill Country, Texas 106
Bayou Cruise, Louisiana 110
Highway 61, Lake Superior, Minnesota 116
Mississippi Great River Road I,
   Minnesota – Missouri 122
Mississippi Great River Road II,
   Tennessee – Louisiana 126
Route 66, Illinois – California 130
Miami to Key West, Florida 136
Blue Ridge Parkway, Virginia – North Carolina ... 142
Dare Trail, North Carolina 148
Cape Cod Route 6A, Massachusetts 152
Mohawk Trail, Massachusetts 158
Connecticut River Byway, Vermont – Massachusetts ... 162
Route 100, Vermont 166
Kancamagus Highway, New Hampshire 170
Mount Washington Auto Road, New Hampshire ... 176

CANADA
Sea to Sky Highway, British Columbia 180
Cabot Trail, Nova Scotia 186

CREDITS   192

INTRODUCTION

FOR THOSE WITH A THIRST FOR ADVENTURE AND THE FREEDOM OF THE OPEN ROAD, NORTH AMERICA IS NIRVANA. The USA alone has some 150 officially designated Scenic Byways of which 31 are All-American Roads – which means they are not simply wonderful roads to travel, but also have unique features that can't be found anywhere else outside of the United States. Every one of these roads has either stunning scenic qualities, important natural features, a fascinating historical heritage, distinct cultural importance, significant archeological value, astounding recreational characteristics, or a mix of any or all of these. Over the border in Canada, the most scenic roads are not officially marked, but that does not make Canadian routes any less interesting or any less deserving of a place on the enthusiastic driver's bucket list. Canada's National Highway System encompasses more than 23,000 miles (37,030 km) of highways (as well as countless more miles of picturesque country roads), and includes some of the most scenic stretches of pavement in the world. From breathtaking ocean views where whales can be spotted breaching to majestic snow-capped peaks, Canada is every bit as good a place to explore by car as its southern neighbor.

The drives featured in this book are among the most breathtaking North America has to offer and have been chosen to present the incredible variety of the natural landscape. Some take the driver along the coast, or along rivers and lakes; many involve high country – whether hills or mountains. Others wind along roads that are wholly inland through scenery that has its own blend of stunning vistas and flavors of North American history.

As a relatively new country, the USA sadly has few extant monuments built by its ancient peoples, whose way of life endured for tens of thousands of years before the arrival of the first European settlers. The nation's more modern history resonates strongly throughout these pages, however. For example, the sights and atmosphere of the California Gold Rush of 1849 can still be glimpsed by driving the Gold Rush Highway 49. Along the route, drivers can experience the untamed and lonely terrain, visit old mines, and experience Wild West saloons and bars. Similarly, Route 66 – taken by thousands in the early 20th century as they sought their fortunes in the west – still symbolizes the essence of the American Dream. Its name alone conjures up magical days gone by, and the hopes and aspirations of all those who traveled across the country in search of a better life in the sunshine. More than any other American road it signifies sheer freedom, and it remains one of the most famous in the world. Route 66 starts at Great Park in Chicago and crosses more than 2,400 miles (3,900 km) of the United States before finishing in Santa Monica on the fabled coast of California. Along the way it crosses three time zones and eight states. Today, with most traffic diverted onto modern interstates, Route 66 is a less-traveled road paved with old dreams and gentle reminders of times long past – but its legend is as powerful as it ever was.

Left: Part of the Cabot Trail, hewn into the side of the hills overlooking Cap Rouge in Nova Scotia, Canada.

Right: Texas Bluebonnets blooming at the Turkey Bend Recreation Area on the Colorado River in Burnet County, Texas.

Following pages: Sunrise over the Mississippi River seen from the Pikes Peak State Park near McGregor in Iowa.

The coastline of the USA is the ninth longest in the world, extending to some 12,380 miles (19,924 km). This pales into insignificance when compared to that of Canada, which has the longest in world, measuring 125,567 miles (202,080 km). It will come as no surprise then that many of the drives featured in the following pages follow a number of superb landscapes where land meets ocean.

One fine example is the journey which includes the Pacific Coast Highway and which runs the length of the USA's West Coast. Second only to Route 66 in fame, this 1,885 mile (2,986 km) drive along the coast of the Pacific Ocean offers an extraordinary diversity of views across ocean and land. It also takes the driver past places of historical and cultural interest, though little can compare to the breathtaking magnificence of the mighty redwood forests that are passed along the way. Another is the route from Miami to Key West, which allows the rare opportunity of driving alongside gliding pelicans. A fascinating engineering feat in its own right, most of this 100 mile (161 km) route takes the car across the long series of bridges and viaducts linking the many islands in the far south of Florida, above the waters that divide the Caribbean Sea from the Gulf of Mexico. Just as arresting, but more rugged, is the ocean-side Cabot Trail in the Canadian province of Nova Scotia. Here, far to the north of balmy Florida, the weather is more extreme, the seas are rougher, and the landscape bleaker. Yet the combination of magnificent ocean views, wonderful highland scenery, and spectacular wildlife – including whales, bald eagles, and moose – is hard to equal.

Away from the oceans, there is no shortage of inland water in either the US or Canada and many spectacular North American drives follow the shores of the continent's rivers and lakes. The Mississippi Great River Road, for example, trails beside the grandest of North American rivers from Lake Itasca in Minnesota to Venice, Louisiana, on the Gulf of

Far left: The Rowena Loops on the Columbia River Highway in Meyer State Park, Oregon.

Above: Stunning view of the Columbia River Gorge where it is overlooked by Vista Point, high on a rocky outcrop.

Mexico, some 2,380 miles (3,832 km) to the south. The longest National Scenic Byway in the USA, it passes through ten states and boasts of being the "Best Drive in America". Elsewhere, adventurous drivers with a taste for beautiful waterways can discover the verdant swamps and shaded bayous (the name means "slow moving stream") west of New Orleans. The Bayou Cruise in Louisiana follows the ancient route of the Mississippi River and offers a heady cocktail of history, scenery, and a mix of Native American, French, Spanish, and Caribbean cultures. A completely different, but equally lovely, experience can be had by driving the Columbia River Scenic Byway in Oregon. Relatively short at just 70 miles (113 km) long, America's first ever scenic byway passes along the Columbia River Gorge, known as one of the Seven Wonders of Oregon thanks to its many waterfalls, unique plant-life, and historic buildings, as well as its astonishing views and panoramic vistas.

Of course, the North American landscape also features vast mountain and upland areas, which also offer myriad opportunities for spectacular driving along routes that wind above the clouds. Among the great highland trips featured in this book is the fabulous Going-to-the-Sun Road, constructed in Montana's Glacier National Park in 1932 to encourage motorists to visit the park and enjoy the 1,583 square miles (4,099 km²) of mountains, lakes, rivers, and wilderness. Over the border in Canada, the Sea-to-Sky Highway runs from Vancouver, at sea level on the Pacific Coast of British Columbia, rising all the way to Whistler in the Rocky Mountains. Originally a logging trail, it was upgraded for the 2010 Olympic Games and is now one of BC's most popular driving roads. Also featured are Pikes Peak in Colorado and the Mount Washington Auto Road in New Hampshire. Both are special; each a single road that rises to the top of a peak. Both are used for motorsport events though readers need not race along them. It is far more enjoyable to take the roads gently and enjoy the incredible views. There are numerous other mountain drives, too, including the San Juan Skyway, the Million Dollar Highway in Colorado, the Pali Highway in Hawaii, the Blue Ridge Parkway from Virginia to North Carolina, and the Kancamagus National Scenic Byway in New Hampshire. All offer different experiences and landscapes, but each is unforgettable in its own way.

Finally, there are the drives which are wholly unique to their special places in the North American landscape. Other great journeys here take the driver across deserts, such as the trip to Death Valley from Las Vegas where Joshua trees rise from the stark terrain. Those looking to follow the footsteps of early pioneers might wish to journey along the New Mexico Turquoise Trail that stretches from Albuquerque to Santa Fe, visiting old mining towns along the route, or drive from Torrey to Bryce Canyon National Park in Utah. Another hauntingly American drive is the evocative, album-cover journey through Monument Valley, on the Colorado Plateau. Here, the scenery is so stunning that no-one could resist the temptation to stop along the way. And while there, those who favor less well-traveled routes might be particularly interested in the 17-mile (27 km) loop on unmade dirt roads that takes drivers into the Navajo Reserve. Stopping to learn about Native American history is highly recommended. Similarly, the Mohawk Trail in Massachusetts also offers tantalizing glimpses of ancient ways and cultures, while the drives through the Hill Country in Texas and along Route 100 in Vermont pass through some of the most exceptional and characteristic scenery to be found anywhere in North America.

There is no one attribute that makes one road trip great and another one dull, but there are very many reasons why every one of the 34 routes described in *North American Road Trips* is special enough to warrant inclusion. Whether the driver is looking for a first-hand experience of history, or unique cultural delights, or simply some of the finest stretches of scenery the world has to offer, these drives offer a bounty of treasure. To enjoy any one of them is a memorable experience but anyone who manages to take a journey along every one of these incredible roads would be very lucky indeed. Hopefully this book will encourage any reader who is able to hop in the car, roll down the windows, and hit the road for an unforgettable journey of a lifetime.

Right: Mount Rohr reflected in the tranquil waters of Duffey Lake on the Sea to Sky Highway in British Columbia, Canada.

Following pages: Lion's Head towers over the Glenn Highway in Alaska.

PALI HIGHWAY
OAHU, HAWAII

The Pali Highway is one of the shortest scenic drives in this collection but a truly memorable one – partly because of the sheer beauty of the views as the road rises through the Ko'olua range of peaks, and partly because this is a journey through the very heart of Hawaiian history and culture.

THE CURRENT ROAD, WHICH STARTS IN HONOLULU ON OAHU'S WESTERN (LEEWARD) COAST AND CROSSES THE ISLAND TO KAILUA ON THE WINDWARD COAST, is actually the third route that has been painstakingly constructed over the years to join the two sides of the island. For hundreds of years there was an ancient footpath over the Nu'uanu Pali, which was one of the very few safe crossings. The first "road", built in 1845, was little more than a track. Importantly though, it allowed horse-drawn carts to make the

crossing for the first time and thus became a vital economic highway for famers bringing produce to Honolulu. In 1898, it was widened and improved. Even back then it was called the Pali Highway, though, in truth, it remained a very narrow road and the trip was one to be undertaken only by the adventurous thanks to the steep ascents and descents, the 22 hairpin bends, and vertiginous drops.

The Old Pali Highway is now closed to all vehicular traffic, though parts of it are still accessible for hikers. Modern day car drivers take the

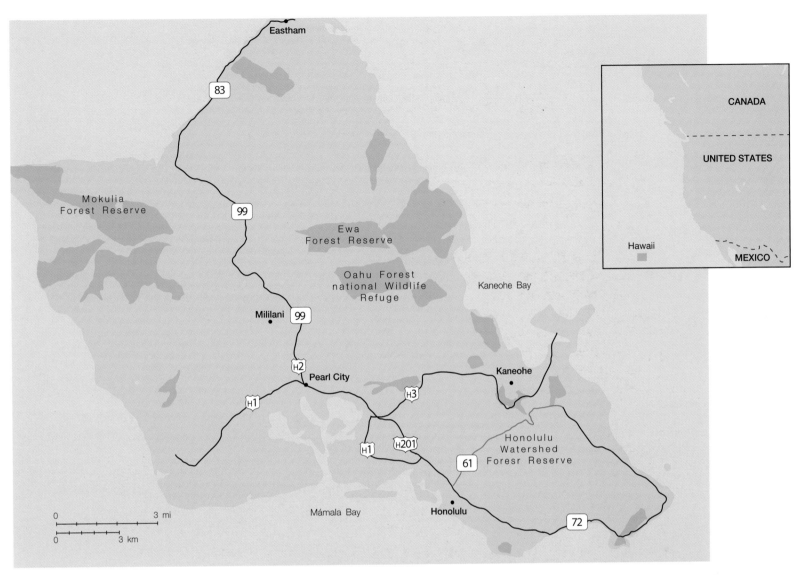

Eastham

83

99

Mokulia
Forest Reserve

Ewa
Forest Reserve

Oahu Forest
national Wildlife
Refuge

Kaneohe Bay

99

Mililani

H2

Pearl City

H1

H3

Kaneohe

H1   H201

61

Honolulu
Watershed
Foresr Reserve

Mámala Bay

Honolulu

72

0   3 mi

0   3 km

CANADA

UNITED STATES

Hawaii

MEXICO

From: Honolulu

To: Kailua

Roads: Highway 61

Distance: 10.8 miles (17.4 km)

Driving Time: Under an hour

When To Go: Year-round

Left: Ancient trees create a tunnel over the
Pali Highway.

Right: The old Pali Highway, first opened in
1845 is now closed to vehicular traffic though
some sections are still accessible for hikers.

new Pali Highway, on which construction started in 1955. As the old highway's builders had found, there were major engineering hurdles to be overcome, notably the boring of two tunnels through the mountains. These were successfully completed and the road – a two-lane highway in each direction – was fully opened in 1961.

Ancient Hawaiian folklore is never far away along the Pali Highway. To the island's native folk the lowlands were the domain of humans; the mountains where the gods lived. These beliefs were respected during construction of the highways over the years and certain large rocks – such as one near Kaheiki, which was believed to guard the house of the gods, and another near Luakaha that protected the waters that lie within the mountains – were left undisturbed. Even today, local legend tells that anyone taking pork over the mountain will be beset by accident while there are also numerous stories of strange apparitions in the heights: white mists that appear suddenly, and ghostly orbs in the night skies.

Some say these are the spirits of the thousands who died during the Battle of Nu'uanu in 1795 when Kamehameha I was busy uniting the Hawaiian islands. Legend suggests that thousands of people, backed up against the Nu'uanu Pali – the sheer cliff that drops into the valley below – were either pushed or chose to jump off. What is certain is that during the construction of the Old Pali Road, some 800 skulls were found.

From downtown Honolulu, the Pali Highway takes travelers through the Nu'uanu residential neighborhood before the rising toward the mountains. Although this is a two-lane highway in both directions, it is not a road designed for speed. The limit is 35 mph (56 km/h) at first, rising to 45 mph (72 km/h) out of town. However, as the road reaches its twistiest sections the limit drops back to just 25 mph (40 km/h).

Very soon, as drivers follow the tree-lined highway, steeply rising mountains come into view. Five miles along the road, don't miss the Pali Lookout on the right. Some 1,000 feet (305 m) above sea-level, this

is one of the few places to stop and admire the amazing views over the island. From here visitors can see right across to the coast, from Kaneohe to Kailua. Offshore are Mokoli'i – known locally as "Chinaman's Hat" – and Coconut Island, home to the University of Hawaii's Institute of Marine Biology. Locals warn tourists to wear a light jacket but not a hat at the lookout as the trade winds which funnel between the mountains can be extremely strong.

Just past the Pali Lookout drivers pass through the two tunnels. On emerging, it's best to slow down as there are a number of sharp bends on the descent. As a bonus, slower speeds allow a better enjoyment of Hawaii's natural beauty and the far-reaching views of the windward shore far below.

All too soon, this magnificent journey comes to an end, passing over some rumble strips before the official terminus of the route at the next junction. Drivers can turn left for Kaneohe, or keep straight on for the beaches of Kailua.

Above: The dramatic view from the Nu'uanu Pali Lookout reaches all the way to the ocean.

Far left: The Pali Lookout is some 1,000 feet (305 m) above sea level on a near-vertical bluff.

MUST SEE

This is a road that reveals the natural beauty of **Oahu island**, offering panoramic views of mountains, sheer cliffs, valleys, and beaches. Clouds and thick verdant forests are also part of the treat.

The one major stop-off place is the **Pali Lookout** where there are amazing views to be had over the valleys to the windward coast. It's also one of the most important historical sites on the island so do not miss it.

HAWAII BELT ROAD
BIG ISLAND, HAWAII

The Big Island of Hawaii is the youngest of the island chain, the biggest by a considerable margin, and the most volcanically active. This circular route offers visions of the island in all its astonishing variety: mountains, rivers, and valleys; active lava flows and older lava deserts; thick forests, acres of wild flowers, and productive green farmlands; and, of course, Hawaii's famous white and black sand beaches.

THE HAWAII BELT ROAD COMPRISES A GRAND LOOP ON ROUTES 11, 19, AND 190, SO VISITORS CAN START AND FINISH WHEREVER IS MOST CONVENIENT. That said, Kona International Airport is just outside Kailua-Kona and seems a reasonable place to start for the purposes of our tour. Worth a visit in Kailua-Kona is the Hulihee Palace, built in 1838 and now a museum containing the massive koa wooden chair built for Princess Ruth, who died in 1883 weighing an impressive 400 lbs (181 kg). The Mokuaikaua Church is also an interesting tourist attraction. This lava rock and coral building was the first Christian church built in Hawaii, in 1820. Nearby is the equally historic Ahuena Heiau, a rebuilt stone structure that was the centerpiece of the capital of the Hawaiian Islands until 1821.

Heading south from Kona, travelers might wish to break the journey at the Kona Coffee Living History Farm, which showcases the luxurious plantation lifestyle enjoyed by the more fortunate of the island's inhabitants in the past. A little further on is a tempting 12-mile (19 km) detour that starts just south of Captain Cook town and loops past the St. Benedict Painted Church, Kealakekua Bay – where Cook was killed in 1779 – and the Pu'uhonua o Honaunau National Park, which offers a taste of Hawaii's history and some of the best snorkeling beaches on the island.

Keep heading toward the south of the island, passing ancient lava fields and lush forests. After Ocean View – one of the fastest-growing communities on the island – the road turns north east, rising on the

Left: St. Benedict's Painted Church was built and painted by the Belgian priest Father John Velghe between 1899 and 1902.

Right: The Chain of Craters road passes a number of extinct volcanoes, and some active ones too – as the lava flow across the road demonstrates.

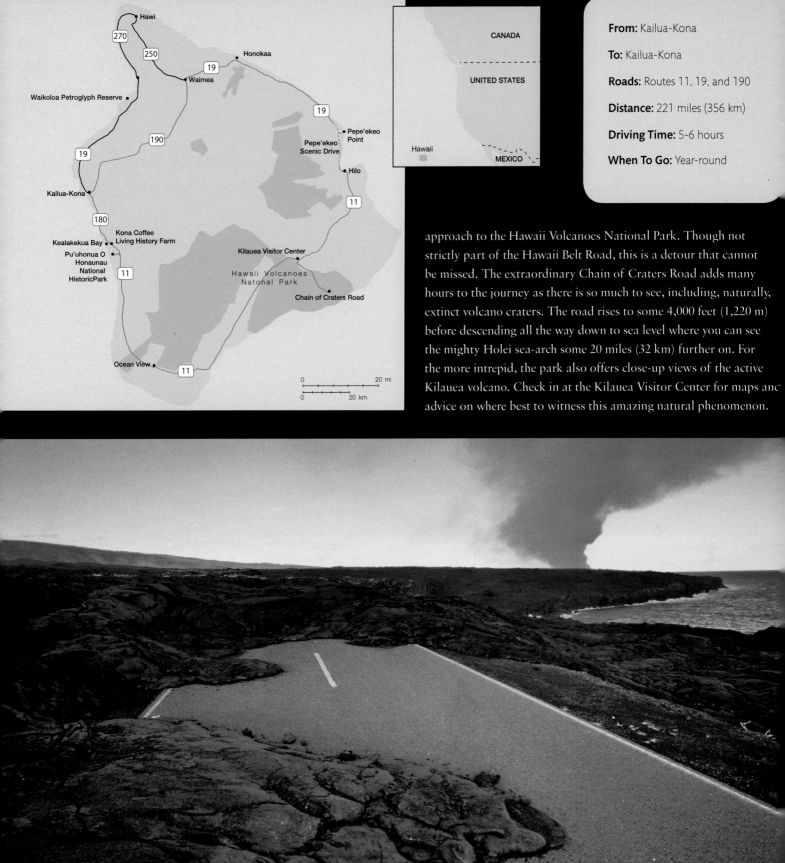

approach to the Hawaii Volcanoes National Park. Though not strictly part of the Hawaii Belt Road, this is a detour that cannot be missed. The extraordinary Chain of Craters Road adds many hours to the journey as there is so much to see, including, naturally, extinct volcano craters. The road rises to some 4,000 feet (1,220 m) before descending all the way down to sea level where you can see the mighty Holei sea-arch some 20 miles (32 km) further on. For the more intrepid, the park also offers close-up views of the active Kilauea volcano. Check in at the Kilauea Visitor Center for maps and advice on where best to witness this amazing natural phenomenon.

Left: The Onomea Falls in the Hawaii Tropical Botanical Gardens – home of some 2,000 different tropical plant species.

Right: One of the most spectacular sights on the route is over the Waipio Valley, some 850 feet (259 m) below the lookout.

Following pages: The extinct Mauna Kea volcano now features astronomical telescopes on its summit.

Back on Route 11, continue toward Hilo, the largest town on the island. Overlooking Hilo Bay, it is located at the feet of the extinct Mauna Kea and the active Mauna Loa and is home to the Tsunami Museum, Pana'ewa Rainforest Zoo, and Banyan Drive where, over the years, celebrities have planted trees to create a famous shaded walkway.

Leave Hilo on Route 19. After Mile 7 another tempting detour arrives, this time along the Pepe'ekeo Scenic Drive, a four mile (6.25 km) section of the old Mamalahoa Highway that winds through thick jungle and offers wonderful views over Onomea Bay. Along the road you will also pass the Hawaii Tropical Botanical Garden, which boasts over 2,000 tropical plant species along its many trails.

At Honokaa, yet another unmissable detour leads to a magnificent panoramic view over the Waipio Valley. Those driving a four-wheel drive vehicle can continue all the way down to the valley floor some 850 feet (259 m) below and on to one of the island's famous black-sand beaches.

Continue to Waimea, a town surrounded by rich farmland and cattle-ranching country. From here a choice of routes opens up. The first option is to take a detour north along the sinuous Kohala Mountain Road (Route 250) to Hawi on the north coast of the island. It's a good choice for anyone looking for great art galleries, restaurants, and bars. The second choice is to stay on the Hawaii Belt which now takes Route 190 back to Kailua-Kona. A third option is continuing on Route 19, a slightly longer coastal route back to the starting point. If taking this

option don't miss the Pu'ukohola Heiau National Historic Site. Here, travelers will find temple ruins dating from around 1580, and the site where Kamehameha I, who unified the island in 1791, built the luakini heiau sacrificial temple.

Still on Route 19, as you get closer to Kona Airport and the end of the journey, look out for signs to the Waikoloa Petroglyph Reserve where there are fascinating ancient carvings in the lava stone, featuring depictions of birds, fish, animals, canoes, and people – remnants of the ancient culture that remains an important aspect of life on the Big Island today.

MUST SEE

The 221 mile (356 km) **Hawaii Belt Road** is easily completed in a few hours, but with so many sights to see most people prefer to measure out the drive in days.

Major attractions along the route include **Kealakekua Bay**, **Pu'uhonua o Honaunau National Park**, **Hawaii Volcanoes National Park**, **Pepe'ekeo Scenic Drive**, and **Pu'ukohola Heiau National Historic Site**.

SEWARD HIGHWAY
ALASKA

The Seward Highway in Alaska is designated a National Forest Scenic Byway, and for good reason: between Anchorage and Seward the route takes in mile after mile of unspoiled landscape where every bend in the road reveals a fresh vista of mountains, coastlines, glaciers, meadows, and valleys.

HEAD SOUTH FROM ANCHORAGE AND ROUTE 1 VERY QUICKLY BECOMES A QUIET TWO-LANE ROAD. Just 10 miles (16 km) out of the city road-trippers can expect to start seeing abundant wildlife and maybe even eagles at Potter Marsh at Mile 117.4 (the markers start at 0 in Seward and finish at 127 in Anchorage). Boardwalks here allow visitors to walk over the marsh to see moose, migratory birds, and spawning salmon.

The entire route is teeming with photogenic scenery, but one viewpoint not to be missed is Beluga Point at Mile 110.5. Named for the white whales that frequent the bay, the parking area has spotting scopes for those who want to watch the great creatures rolling in the waves. Bird Creek (Mile 101) is another superb spot for photography and for watching fishermen hooking salmon. Soon after, at Bird Point – which overlooks Turnagain Arm at Mile 96 – there is another excellent lookout for beluga whales. Visit at the right time and it's possible to witness the tidal bores that rush up the inlet at high tide when the ocean's tidal waters surge over the river waters coming downstream.

Named for Colonel James Girdwood, who staked four gold claims at nearby Crow Creek, Girdwood at Mile 90 boasts a wide expanse of summer wildflowers. Close by is Mount Alyeska, the busiest ski resort in Alaska. In summer, visitors can still take the ski tram that whisks them to 2,300 feet (701 m) up the flower-covered slopes. The fare is worth it for the magnificent panoramic views alone, but anyone making the scent is also likely to see local wildlife including bears and marmots as well as glaciers and snow-covered mountain peaks.

Right: The Seward Highway runs along the north coast of the Turnagain Arm with the snow-covered Alaska range in the background.

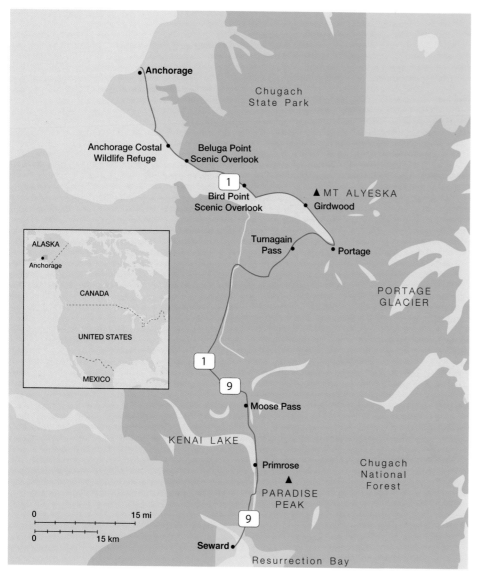

From: Anchorage

To: Seward

Roads: Route 1 then Route 9

Distance: 127 miles (204 km)

Driving Time: 3 hours

When To Go: Best in summer

It's worth taking a detour along the Portage Glacier Road to Portage Valley. Along this route, visitors can discover what happened to the forest when, after an earthquake in 1964, seawater covered the area and soaked into the soil. The sight of the dead trees is offset by views of the many glaciers above. At Boggs Visitor Center visitors can take a boat ride on Portage Lake that has a special permit to get up close to the glacier. From the deck, icebergs that have broken off the Portage Glacier can be seen.

Back on the Seward Highway the road rises to Turnagain Pass and for the next 40 miles (65 km) or so the scenery is an unbroken vista of mountains and lakes. Look out for Canyon Creek, where gold was once found, Jerome Lake, Tern Lake, and the much bigger Kenai Lake. The latter is particularly popular with photographers because its deep blue-green waters, formed from glacial melt-water, reflect the snow-capped mountains above. There are plenty of parking areas along the lake.

At Mile 56.4, road-trippers can take another detour to Hope, one of the first gold mining settlements in Alaska. Much was destroyed during the 1964 earthquake but there are still plenty of original wooden buildings to be seen.

Moose Pass, a small town apparently so-named because a moose once obstructed the postman's dog team in 1903, has a giant waterwheel

to which a sharpening stone has been attached. Visitors can sharpen their pocket knives while contemplating a sign that reads: "Moose Pass is a peaceful little town. If you have an axe to grind, do it here". Beyond Moose Pass, the scenery opens up again. Check out Snow River at Mile 14, where trees, streams, and gravel beds are overlooked by the ice fields of Paradise Peak.

At the end of the route is Seward, which is home to a vibrant harbor surrounded by great fish restaurants. Behind are the Marathon Mountains and just beyond is the magnificent Resurrection Bay which remains ice-free even in winter. Take a Kenai Fjords boat trip from here to see killer whales, sea otters, seals, sea lions, and much more.

Far left: The still water of Kenai Lake, viewed from Slaughter Ridge in Cooper Landing.

Above: The port at Seward with the Marathon Mountains in the distance.

Below: A Humpback Whale breaches in the Kenai Fjord.

Following pages: Surfers take advantage of the tidal bore in the Turnagain Arm which can reach up to 10 feet (3 m) in height and travel at up to 15 mph (24 km/h).

MUST SEE

The seashore at Turnagain Arm is a must, as this is the USA's second highest tide at 37 feet (11.2 meters). At low tide there are miles of mudflats, while high tide often creates 6 foot (2 meters) bore waves.

The park at **Kenai Peninsula Borough** offers glaciers, rivers, rugged coast and forests and here you can fish for giant salmon or spot whales and sea lions. **Bird Point** is another whale-watching option, as belugas feed from early summer to September. **Mount Alveska** offers the chance to spot black bears. And don't miss **Resurrection Bay** in Seward where humpback whales, sea lions, seals, porpoises and even killer whales can be seen.

ANCHORAGE TO VALDEZ
ALASKA

*The Glenn Highway runs 328 miles (528 km) from Anchorage to the Tok Junction,
though this journey turns south onto the Richardson Highway at the Hub of Alaska
at Mile 189 (304 km) taking the route to the historic town of Valdez.*

LEAVE ANCHORAGE ON THE GLENN HIGHWAY (AK-1) AND
CONSIDER MAKING A FIRST STOP AT THE EAGLE RIVER
NATURE CENTER where you can walk in the Chugach State Park with
its massive cliffs and many waterfalls. The park also contains Thunder
Bird Falls, which can be accessed further along the route (a short hike
is necessary) and seen from a deck that offers great views. Not far from
the cascade is Eklutna. Native Americans are believed to have lived in
the area for some 800 years but Eklutna Village, dating back to 1650, is

the area's oldest continuously inhabited Athabaskan Indian settlement.
It also features St. Nicholas Church, built by Russian Orthodox
missionaries in the early 1880s.

There are many spectacular glaciers along this route but the
Matanuska Glacier at Mile 101 (162.5 km) is the largest in the state
accessible by road. It is also possible to take a boat trip here, and float
along the river while taking in views of the abundant wildlife. The best
free views of the glacier, which is 27 miles (43 km) long by 4 miles (6.4 km)

From: Anchorage

To: Valdez

Roads: Route 1 then Route 9

Distance: 299 miles (481 km)

Driving Time: 5-6 hours

When To Go: Best in summer

Below: Alaska is a land of mountains, glaciers, and waterways.

Above: The Trans-Alaska oil pipeline can be seen at a number of places along the route.

wide, are from the Matanuska Glacier State Recreation Site, or from a small parking area a mile further on. Anyone who wants to get up really close can drive on to Mile 102 (164 km), where for $30 per person you can enter the Matanuska Glacier Park. There, cars can drive right up and park next to the glacier, though you'll have to get out to walk on the ice!

At Mile 103 (166 km) is the famous Lion's Head, the rocky outcrop next to the Matanuska Glacier that's been made famous in thousands of publicity photographs. It's possible to hike up the Lion's Head and from the top there are wonderful views over the glacier, the Matanuska River, and Caribou Creek – all overlooked by the Talkeetna and Chugach mountains.

From here the road passes Jackass Creek – where many like to stop and have a photograph taken by the sign – before climbing to Eureka Summit, the highest point on the highway. Next is the town of Glenallen, home to many of the workers on the massive Prudhoe Bay to Valdez oil pipeline project while it was under construction in the 1970s. Along

the route you will see the Trans-Alaska pipeline at various points, including some of the pump stations that keep the oil flowing through the 800 mile (1288 km) pipe.

After Glenallen, turn south onto the Richardson Highway (AK-4). This is Alaska's oldest highway, first built as a track from Valdez to Eagle in 1898. It was improved after the Fairbanks Gold Rush in 1910 though it remained unsuitable for vehicles until the 1920s and wasn't actually made into a paved road until 1957.

At first, the road follows the route of the Copper River below three impressive peaks in the Wrangell Mountains – Mount Sanford on the left, Mount Drum in the center, and Mount Wrangell on the left. About 58 thousand years ago this whole area was underwater. Glaciers further downstream blocked the river and created the massive and long-gone Lake Ahtna.

Milepost 16. Should the weather be poor at the time of your trip – the Pacific coastal area can be very overcast in winter – it is worth taking a detour to the top of the Cleator Road, which usually remains above cloud level. On clear days, this vantage point has magnificent views over the San Juan Islands and Bellingham Bay.

At Milepost 18 some of the route's best views of Chuckanut Bay, Chuckanut Island, to Clark's Point can be found, after which the road takes drivers along the Old Fairhaven Parkway and the final destination of Bellingham. There is much to enjoy at the end of this beautiful road trip. The Victorian architecture of Fairhaven's Historic District on the south edge of Bellingham Bay exudes old-world charm, making this another must-see for anyone looking for a flavor of the area's heritage. Fairhaven Park offers walks along the shores of Padden Creek, while the more adventurous can take a foot ferry from here to the San Juan Islands.

MUST SEE

Most of this route features fabulous views over the **Pacific coast**, but visitors greedy for more should make time to visit the **Bat Caves** and hike the **Oyster Dome Trail**. Both offer superb sightseeing. There also are a number of splendid seafood restaurants along the route including the **Oyster Bar** and the **Oyster Creek Inn**.

A stop at **Taylor Shellfish Farms** is also highly recommended. Close by, 55 million-year-old fossils can be found at **Milepost 12**. **Larrabee State Park** is a popular recreation area while **Fairhaven's park** and **historic district** are both well worth a visit.

Below: Erosion over the millennia has created strange sandstone formations in Larrabee State Park. The San Juan Islands are in the distance.

GOLD RUSH TRAIL
CALIFORNIA

In 1849, gold was discovered at Sutter's Mill, California. The find led to thousands of hopeful prospectors streaming into the state from all over the world. Known as the '49ers (Highway 49 takes its name from them), they staked claims, dug, and panned for riches while other enterprising folk built the saloons, hotels, and brothels that developed into a string of mining towns.

MANY OF THESE STILL EXIST AND ARE BOTH HISTORIC AND PICTURESQUE PLACES TO VISIT. After Sutter's Mill, gold was found at Woods Creek, then at Mariposa, and at countless other places in and around the rivers and creeks in the foothills of the Sierra Nevada mountains. Before long a stagecoach route was established, and that same route today forms the basis of Highway 49 – the Gold Rush Trail.

At 326-miles- (525-km-) long, the Gold Rush Trail could be driven in a single day but most people choose to take longer in order to appreciate the sights of this wonderful route. It not only offers a unique insight into Wild West heritage (though there are plenty of sites where travelers can learn about gold panning, the Gold Rush, and the steam railways) but also some of the best wine tasting in California, along with hiking,

fishing, boating, and even skiing in winter. Better still, there's an ever-changing vista along the route. Highway 49 is where natural beauty and America's history come together and a drive along the Gold Rush Trail is to be transported into an unchanging American landscape of meadows, rivers, creeks, and lakes; oaks, pines, firs, and redwoods; rocky ravines and waterfalls. Along the route are towns where the architecture recalls the heady days of gold fever.

Given the length of Highway 49, it's impossible to mention every worthwhile stop, but there are a number that are simply unmissable. Starting in Oakhurst in the south, first up is Mariposa – home to the

Below: Main Street in the beautifully preserved town of Columbia, once an important mining town.

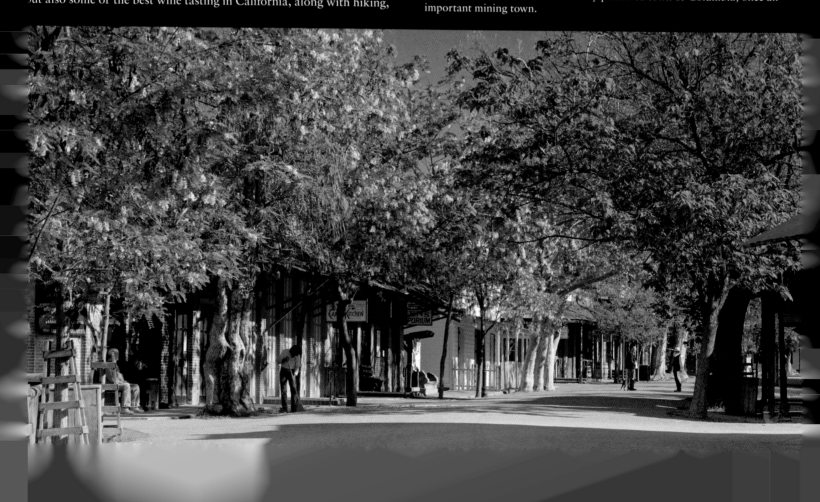

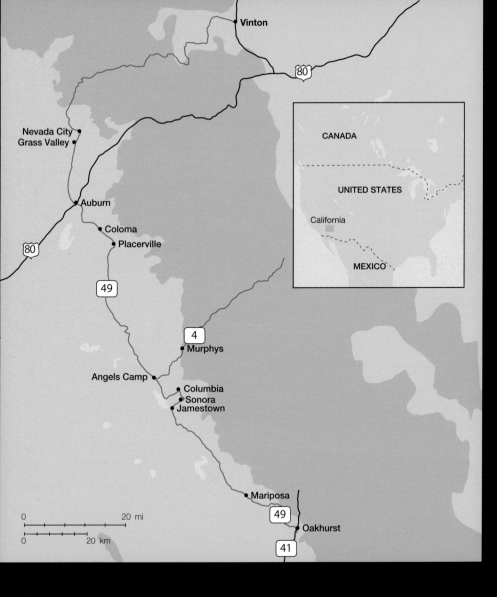

From: Oakhurst

To: Vinton

Roads: AC Highway 49

Distance: 326 miles (525 km)

Driving Time: 8-10 hours

When To Go: Year round

Below: The old Tuolumne County Courthouse in Sonora – the town known as the "Queen of the Mother Lode".

California State Mining and Mineral Museum and the Mariposa Museum and History Center, both of which provide fascinating details of Gold Rush history as well as the Native American traditions of the area.

Railtown 1897 State Historic Park in Jamestown might look familiar, as it has featured in over 200 films and TV shows. This railroad museum is open every day and at weekends steam-train rides are on offer. Look out, too, for the stone marker a mile north of Jamestown at Woods Creek, which is where the second of California's gold discoveries was made.

The town of Sonora – known as the "Queen of the Mother Lode" – is the largest town along the route. Look out for the courthouse, which is still in use and virtually unchanged since it was built in the 19th century. A little further north (road-trippers will need to detour from Highway 49) is Columbia. In its heyday, this was a massive mining town. Today, it is a great place to learn about the history of the Gold Rush and soak up the authentic atmosphere of those long gone days. There are more historic buildings in Columbia than anywhere else along the route, all preserved as part of the Columbia State Historic Park.

Left: The town of Auburn whose well-preserved town center provides a strong flavor of the old Wild West.

Below: The historic covered bridge, built in 1862, spanning the South Yuba River at Bridgeport.

on what he called "Jackass Hill". A replica cabin now marks the spot. A little further along, wine lovers might wish to take a short detour along Highway 4 to Murphys. Once a lawless mining town, it is now an important, and affluent, center of the Sierra wine industry.

Placerville is also a great place to stop. At Hangtown's Gold Bug Park travelers will find the only gold mine in the state where it is possible to explore the underground tunnels (guided tours are available). The nearby El Dorado County Historical Museum also has an excellent collection of Native American and Gold Rush artifacts on show.

Sutter's Mill, near Coloma, is where the Gold Rush began and a tour of the mill at the Marshall Gold Discovery State Historic Park is highly recommended. Here, you can see the exact spot where James Marshall found the first specks of gold back in 1849. A little further along the route is Auburn, another Gold Rush town with a well-preserved historic center that immerses visitors in the atmosphere of the old Wild West. Grass Valley is home to the Empire Mine State Historic Park – the site of

There are numerous well-preserved gold mining towns along this route, including **Sonora**, **Angels Camp**, **Columbia**, and **Nevada City**. Learn about the history of the **Gold Rush** at museums in **Mariposa**, **Jamestown**, **Sutter's Mill**, and **Placerville**.

one of the oldest and biggest mines in California. At Bridgeport in the South Yuba River State Park (which is worth another detour) you can see the historic covered bridges that were constructed in the 19th century.

Nevada City makes an excellent overnight stop for its great shops and restaurants. You can also visit the world's biggest hydraulic mine at the Malakoff Diggins State Historic Park, or, for a little culture, visit the Nevada Theatre where Mark Twain often gave lectures. The Gold Rush Trail ends in Vinton, where Frenchman Lake offers boating, fishing, and camping for those in need of a rest at the end of a stunning journey.

PACIFIC COAST HIGHWAY I
WASHINGTON – CALIFORNIA

The Pacific Coast Highway from the Olympic National Park in Washington State near Seattle all the way south to San Diego on the Mexican border, is one of the great American drives. It's a journey that can be done on the Interstate 5, which runs parallel to the ocean but never provides even a glimpse of it. But far better is to take more time and drive Highway 101 which offers everything from the verdant green forests of Washington, to the stunning vistas of Big Sur through to the wonderful beaches of Southern California. What's more, for much of the way the route is relatively uncrowded, the varied countryside relatively undeveloped, and there are numerous well-preserved historical sites to visit.

From: Olympic National Park, Washington State

To: San Francisco, California

Roads: US-101, US-1

Distance: 1,245 miles (2,004 km)

Driving Time: 26 hours

When To Go: Year-round

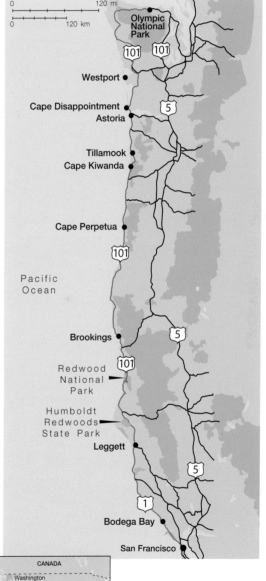

STARTING IN PORT TOWNSEND, FOLLOW US-101 ROUND THE OLYMPIC PENINSULA CLOSE TO THE MOST NORTH-WESTERN POINT OF CONTINENTAL USA as you drive through the Olympic National Park, a land of dense timber, rivers, and streams.

After the Quinault Indian Reservation you might want to take a detour to Westport, dubbed the "Salmon Capital of the World", where migrating grey whales are often seen. A little further on, South Bend on Willapa Bay calls itself the "Oyster Capital of the World".

Continue south to Cape Disappointment where the Columbia River meets the Pacific Ocean, then cross the 4.1 mile (6.6 km) Astoria-Megler bridge – the longest continuous truss bridge in the USA – across the Columbia River and into Oregon.

From Astoria – one of the very earliest settlements in western USA – US-101 follows the Oregon Coast for some 365 miles (588 km), providing limitless views of rocks, beaches, and the wild Pacific seas. It's especially dramatic south of Cannon Beach, where the road runs 700 feet (213 m) above the ocean and is overlooked by the even higher Neahkahnie Mountain inland.

Above: This is the Avenue of the Giants, a stretch of massive Humbolt Redwood trees which create stunning avenues in the drive through the Humbolt Redwoods State Park.

Far left: The Golden Gate Bridge on the approach to San Francisco may be a world-renowned landmark but it remains a breathtaking sight. Walkways are open in daylight hours for walkers and cyclists seeking the finest views of San Francisco Bay.

Between Tillamook and Lincoln City US-101 heads inland, so it's worth taking the 35 mile (56 km) Three Capes Loop to keep on the oceanfront and see the 1890 lighthouse and strange Sitka spruce – the Octopus Tree – in Cape Meares State Park. This section of road is also another prime whale-watching area. And don't miss Cape Kiwanda with its raging surf and 327 foot (100 m) standing rock stack some half a mile offshore.

Cape Perpetua, the Hecata Head Lighthouse, and the Sealion Caves just south of there are all worth visits before continuing down US-101 to Brookings and over the state line and into California.

Stretching for nearly 1,000 miles (1,610 km), California seems to have it all for the visitor: from the Redwood forests in the north, to the metropolitan excitement of San Francisco, past the beauty of Big Sur,

Above: North Head Lighthouse at Cape Disappointment where the Columbia River meets the Pacific Ocean.

Right: The Olympic National Park is a land of lumber, rivers, streams, and mountains. This is the road below Steeple Rock.

Carmel and Monterey, to the elegance of Santa Barbara, and on to the mega-city of Los Angeles, and then further to San Diego on the Mexican border. In Northern California the Jedediah Smith Redwoods State Park or the Redwood National Park – home of the world's tallest tree, the 370 foot (113 m) Libbey Tree – is a must. Further south, you will drive through the Humbolt Redwoods State Park, otherwise known as the "Avenue of the Giants".

After the town of Leggett take US-1 to continue along the coast as US-101 heads inland for a while. Pass Bodega Bay, the Point Reyes National Seashore, Stinson Beach, and Mount Tamalpais, then over the mighty Golden Gate Bridge and into San Francisco. You can park at either end of the 1.7 mile (2.7 km) long bridge whose sidewalks are open to walkers, cycles, and wheelchairs during daylight hours.

Once in San Francisco, Pier 39 with its restaurants, shops, bars, stunning views of the harbor, and basking sealions, is a must for most visitors. The old prison on Alcatraz Island, where Al Capone and other famous convicts were held, is now a major attraction. And among a host of other attractions are the famous cable cars, Lombard Street ("the world's crookedest"), and the San Francisco Zoo with its thousands of endangered animals.

MUST SEE

The whole point of taking the **Pacific Coast Highway** is to enjoy the constantly changing coastal vistas but along the way there is also so much to see and do.

The Olympic National Park itself is beautiful and undeveloped, while once you get into **Oregon** the coast gets much more rugged and wilder and here there are plenty of **whale-watching** opportunities.

Don't miss **Cape Perpetua** and the **Sealion Caves**, nor, further south, the **Redwood National Park**. Then make sure you leave plenty of time to enjoy the delights of **San Francisco**.

PACIFIC COAST HIGHWAY II
CALIFORNIA

The Pacific Coast Highway running south from San Francisco to San Diego on the Mexican border is a wonderful 610 miles (982 km) cruise down US-1 which never strays far from the coastline. Drive past Half Moon Bay and skirt Big Basin Redwoods State Park until you reach the resort of Santa Cruz with its famous boardwalk featuring rides, wooden carousels, and roller coasters.

FURTHER SOUTH ARE NUMEROUS REMINDERS OF THIS AREA'S SPANISH AND MEXICAN PAST, especially around Monterey, the former capital of California, and Carmel with its famous mission. In Monterey, don't miss Cannery Row down by the waterfront where the old canning factories have been turned into fine restaurants and bars. Nor Monterey's justly famous aquarium.

From here, take a detour around the 17-Mile Drive toll road past the famous golf resorts of Spanish Bay and Pebble Beach then take time out in Carmel (where Clint Eastwood was once mayor) for its designer boutiques and art galleries. The Carmel Mission with its beautiful gardens are also well worth a visit. Running 90 miles (145 km) south of Carmel is Big Sur, a fabulous stretch of coastline that has mostly

Above: The Big Sur Coastline south of Carmel offers some of the finest scenery in California. This is the Bixby Bridge overlooking the Pacific Ocean.

Left: The boardwalk at Santa Cruz with its many fairground rides and roller coasters.

remained wholly undeveloped. US-1 was only constructed through the mountains that rise out of the Pacific Ocean in 1937 and it has remained unspoilt ever since. Stop wherever and whenever you can for wonderful views and picture opportunities.

The mountains become more open ranch land at the southern end of Big Sur and here you will find the town of San Simeon and its most famous landmark, Hearst Castle. Built by William Randolph Hearst, the newspaper magnate depicted by Orson Welles in *Citizen Kane* in the early 20th century, it's an extraordinary monument to one man's megalomania, but the house and gardens are nevertheless well worth a visit.

About half way between San Francisco and Los Angeles is San Luis Obispo, site of another famous old Mission house. The town is now a buzzing place with many students, fine beaches, and a very lively downtown district.

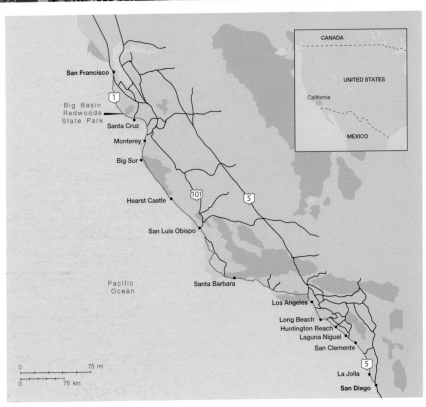

Keep on down US-1 to Santa Barbara, a town that looks more like a Mediterranean than a Californian place thanks to the fact that after an earthquake in 1929 it was rebuilt entirely in a mission-era architectural style. Great beaches, a busy wharf area, loads of fine restaurants, and the "Queen of Missions", Mission Santa Barbara, make this an essential stop.

From here, continue past Malibu and cross Los Angeles (US-1 becomes the I-10 Santa Monica Freeway for a while, but take Lincoln Boulevard to regain US-1 past Venice and Los Angeles Airport). The road crosses LAX which provides the weird experience of watching 747s taxiing overhead.

Pass Long Beach, Huntington Beach, and Newport Beach (diverting to Disneyland if you wish) and continue south toward Laguna Beach. The Crystal Cove State Park is a fine stretch of coastline with miles of beaches and well-marked trails for hikers. Continue to San Clemente, where the "Western White House", President Richard Nixon's former home is located.

MUST SEE

The **boardwalk** of **Santa Cruz**, downtown **San Luis Obispo**, the Spanish-style architecture of **Santa Barbara**, and the wonderfully upmarket resort of **La Jolla** are all worth enjoying on this drive.

In the greater **Los Angeles** area, **Venice Beach**, **Hollywood**, **Disneyland**, and **Long Beach** all offer plenty of tourist attractions.

But perhaps the finest stops on this route are the **old mission towns** of **Monterey** and **Carmel**, **17-Mile Drive** around the **Del Monte** peninsula, and the truly stunning scenery of **Big Sur**.

Right: San Diego's Balboa Park is just one of the attractions at the end of the Pacific Highway.

Below: Fisherman's Wharf in Monterey, where the old fish canning factories reach right down to the water's edge.

The road south is now designated I-5 and takes you to La Jolla, the upmarket coastal area of San Diego which has fine shops and many great cafes, bars, and restaurants on the cliffs that overlook the Pacific Ocean. Nearby Windansea offers some of the best surfing along the coast while the Museum of Contemporary Art offers more artistic pleasures.

From here it's a short drive to downtown San Diego, a city that revolves around the massive US Navy base but which also boasts Balboa Park and the famous San Diego Zoo, one of the world's largest. As far as the Pacific Highway is concerned, San Diego represents the end of the road and it also represents the end of the USA as just south of the city is the Mexican border and – just beyond – the Mexican city of Tijuana.

From: San Francisco

To: San Diego

Roads: US-1, US-5

Distance: 610 miles (982 km)

Driving Time: 14 hours

When To Go: Year-round

HIGHWAY 120 OVER THE SIERRA NEVADA AND THE TIOGA PASS
CALIFORNIA

There are many passes over the top of the Sierra Nevada mountain range in California. Perhaps the most extreme is the Rubicon Trail between Lake Tahoe and Sacramento, but that route can only be undertaken by experienced off-roaders in modified 4x4s. Of the passes open to ordinary cars, the obvious choice is Highway 120. Not only does this route take in the highest pass, but it also takes travelers through spectacular Yosemite Park.

THE JOURNEY STARTS IN MANTECA, IN CALIFORNIA'S
GRAND CENTRAL VALLEY, and follows Highway 120 to Escalon,
an old railway town with an interesting Historical Museum. From there,
road trippers should continue to Oakdale, cross the Stanislaus River, and
head into the "Cowboy Capital of the World" with its Cowboy Museum,
Rodeo, and some of the oldest Wild West buildings in the state. Some
12.5 miles (20 km) further on is a turn on the left to Knights Ferry, which
is well worth a stop. This old Gold Rush town boasts the longest covered
bridge west of the Mississippi, as well as the oldest general store in the
state. From here the road climbs toward the foothills of the Sierra Nevada
and for the next 80 miles (128 km) or so there are no major towns. Keep
on the 120 toward Yosemite National Park and eventually you will reach
Chinese Camp, one of the Gold Rush towns that sprang up in the 1880s.
Visitors can still see the Wells Fargo Bank where miners weighed and
deposited their gold.

After passing Lake Don Pedro the road continues to rise. Road
trippers can choose to take either "New Priest Grade" or the shorter,
but steeper, "Old Priest Grade" – the original Native-American path

From: Manteca

To: Benton Station

Roads: Highway 120

Distance: 224 miles (361 km)

Driving Time: 5 hours

When To Go: Best in summer, closed
November to May/June

Far left: The top of the Half Dome, seen from Olmstead Point
in the heart of the Yosemite National Park.

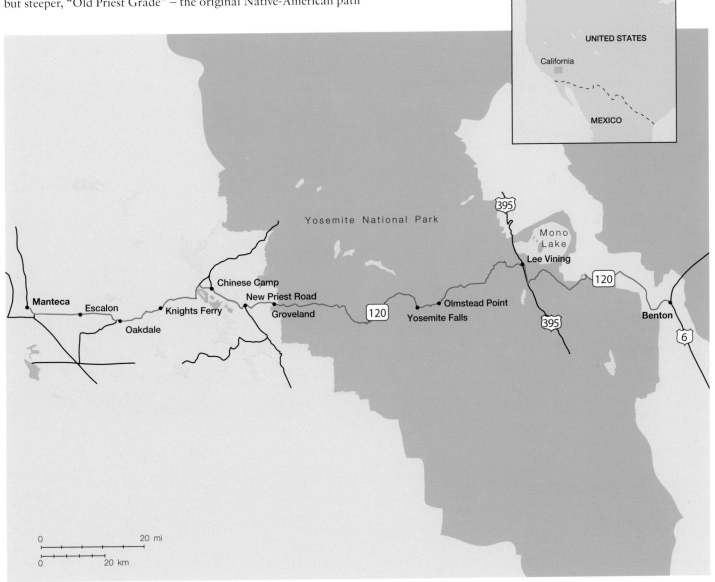

and mule train road. Both meet at the top of Priest Station after which the road passes through Big Oak Flat, then on to Groveland, one of the largest of the old Gold Rush towns. Notable sights here include the historic jailhouse and Iron Door Grille, listed as a California Historical Landmark.

After leaving Groveland, make time to stop at Buck Meadows to visit Rainbow Fall and Pool and take in the sights at the Rim of the World viewing point. It overlooks the Tuolumne River Canyon, which is popular with white water rafters.

From here travelers enter the Yosemite National Park, one of the USA's great natural treasures and the first area set aside for the public to enjoy by President Lincoln as far back as the Civil War. When buying a ticket to enter the park, trippers can also pick up maps and advice for what to see and do. Fortunately, two of the three groves of Giant Sequoia trees in Yosemite are on the route of Highway 120 and won't require a detour.

Continuing along 120, after passing Yosemite Creek then Tenaya Lake drivers will join the Tioga Road which starts at Big Oak and Crane Flat Junction, an area of thick forest. It rises through far more rugged country to 9,945 feet (3,031 m) in the high, snow-covered Sierra Nevada. As the Tioga Road follows the contours of the Sierra Nevada

Right: Giant Sequoia trees in the Yosemite National Park – two of the three groves of these magnificent trees can be seen from Highway 120.

Below: Mono Lake covers some 70 square miles and is home to the unusual Tufas Towers rock formations that rise out of the lake's still waters.

Following pages: The stunning Yosemite Valley – carved by glacier millions of years ago. It's some 7.5 miles (12 km) long and 3000-3500 feet (915-1067 m.) deep.

high country, the trees give way to mountain views of Mount Clark and Mount Hoffman.

Further up the road is Olmsted Point, from which there are magnificent views of the Tanaya Canyon and Tanaya Lake. Sightseers will also want to view the series of granite domes and mountains such as Polly Dome, Half Dome, and Clouds Rest. Clouds Rest is particularly impressive, standing at 9,926 feet (3,025 m) above sea level and towering nearly 5,000 feet (1,525 m) over Tanaya Creek. It's worth stopping here to take the short trail that offers stunning views of Tanaya Peak, Tanaya Lake, and Mount Conness. More experienced hikers have a choice of numerous other trails from this point. Tanaya Lake itself is the largest in the Yosemite Park and was named after Chief Tanaya, leader of the Ahwahnechee tribe. It's now an important watersports venue, offering fishing, sailing, canoeing, and kayaking. Its sandy beach also makes a fine picnic venue.

Some eight miles (13 km) further up the road is Tuolumne Meadows, an area of relatively flat land alongside the sinuous Tuolumne River. In summer it's a riot of wildflowers and from here there's a tough hike to Elizabeth Lake at 9,500 feet (2,850 m).

Keep driving east on the Tioga Road and you'll be rewarded with stunning views of Lembert Dome, a large white granite formation. It

Above: Tenaya Lake in the alpine region between Yosemite Valley and Tuolumne Meadows. This "Jewel of the High Country" is at an elevation of 8,150 feet (2,484 m).

Right: The Tioga Pass road is an example of extreme road-building engineering as it rises to 9,945 feet (3,031 m.).

Left: Lupine and Indian Paintbrush wild flowers brighten the Tuolumne Meadows.

MUST SEE

Highway 120 started out as the **Big Oak Flat Road** – used by mining prospectors on the way to the **Sierra Nevada Mountains** – and the various **Gold Rush towns** along the route should not be missed.

The main attractions, however, are **Giant Sequoia trees**, **Yosemite Falls**, **Olmstead Point**, and the summit of the **Tioga Pass** in **Yosemite National Park**. Though the total driving time for Highway 120 is around five hours, most people spend a few days on the road as there is so much to see and do.

can be climbed with care, though it's reputed to be very windy near the top. Continue toward the Tioga Pass and view Mount Dana and Mount Gibbs on the right hand side.

Once travelers have climbed to 9,945 feet (3,031 m.) they will have arrived at the highest point, the Tioga Pass, named for a Native-American term meaning "where it forks". This is the highest point in California accessible to cars. From the top the road descends quickly once it leaves Yosemite Park and leads to Lee Vining where Highway 120 meets the I-395 and the Tioga Road ends. However, before leaving the area it's worth visiting the nearby Mono Lake which covers an area of more than 70 square miles (180 km²). Here road-trippers will see great flocks of migratory birds and the strange Tufas Towers rock formations that rise from the waters of the lake.

Take I-395 about five miles (8 km) south, then rejoin Highway 120 as it climbs the Mono Lake Basin Road. Along here is the largest stand of Jeffrey Pine trees in the USA. Soon after the road arrives in Benton Hot

Springs, a once thriving town thanks to the natural hot springs that are claimed to have therapeutic effects. Now, the marker as you enter town puts its total population as 13½. From here it is just 3.5 miles (5.6 km) to Benton Station, the end of the route where Highway 120 meets Highway 6.

Above: The Lembert Dome is a granite rock formation that rises some 800 feet (240 m.) above Tuolumne Meadows and the Tuolumne River.

Right: Wonderful views on a clear day at the highest point of the Tioga Pass.

Following pages: Sunset illuminates the Half Dome as it dominates the Merced River in Yosemite National Park.

COLUMBIA RIVER
SCENIC BYWAY
OREGON

The Columbia River starts high in the Canadian Rocky Mountains. Over the course of its 1,200 mile (1,930 km) journey to the Pacific Ocean countless other rivers and streams join it, swelling the watercourse so that it becomes the fourth-largest river in the USA. Today, Columbia River Gorge is known as one of the Seven Wonders of Oregon – thanks to its many waterfalls, unique plant life, historic buildings, and myriad panoramic vistas. Winding through this superb environment, the Columbia River Scenic Byway in Oregon was the first scenic byway to be established in the USA, and remains one of the greatest drives the nation has to offer.

STARTING FROM THE HISTORIC DOWNTOWN AREA OF TROUTDALE, FOLLOW THE KEYSTONE-SHAPED SIGNS THROUGH SPRINGDALE TO THE SMALL TOWN OF CORBETT. Following the byway drivers will soon arrive at the Portland Women's Forum Scenic Viewpoint where many make their first stop. Here, there are simply breath-taking views over the gorge and the scenic Vista House, perched high up on a rocky outcrop overlooking the river below. It is to these views that the route owes its existence. When engineer Samuel Lancaster and railroad entrepreneur Samuel Hill saw the

view from Chanticleer Point (now the Portland Women's Forum Scenic Viewpoint) early in the 20th century, they vowed to create a scenic drive along the course of the river, a task that involved tunneling through immensely-hard basalt rock, building roads that clung to sheer cliffs, and constructing numerous bridges.

The first sections of the road were opened in 1916. Soon after, in 1918, the beautifully designed Vista House was built as an observatory at Crown Point. A mile (1.6 km) after the first scenic stop, it now serves as a museum. Visitors can learn about Oregon's pioneering history as well as how the highway was constructed all those years ago. In addition, since the Vista House is perched some 733 feet (223 m) above the river, it offers yet more astonishing views.

The next section of the route is a paradise for waterfall lovers. The following five miles (8 km) of road feature numerous of cascades, some of which can be seen from the comfort of the driver's seat. Others require drivers to stop and make a short hike for the best views and photo opportunities. Wahkeena Falls can be viewed from the road, though it is well worth parking up to appreciate the sight. Multnomah Falls, one of the USA's tallest at 620 feet (189 m) comes into view soon after. One of the most popular attractions along this drive, it is highly recommended that visitors break the drive here for a walk up to Benson Bridge, which crosses the falls, or the longer climb up to the very top.

A little further along the road are Horsetail Falls, near the road, and Ponytail Falls, another short walk from the highway. Continue until you reach the Bonneville Lock and Dam – a National Historic Landmark. You can learn about its construction and operation at either of the two visitor centers.

Keep driving east along 1-84 until you pass the Bridge of the Gods, a massive cantilever bridge whose 1,858 foot (566 m) span connects Oregon with Washington State. Further along the road is Cascade Locks, which, until the construction of the Bonneville Dam, allowed steamboats to

Above: A paddle-wheel tourist boat entering the Lock at the Bonneville Lock and Dam.

Far left: A stunning view of the Columbia River Gorge and the Vista House perched on the rocks overlooking the river below.

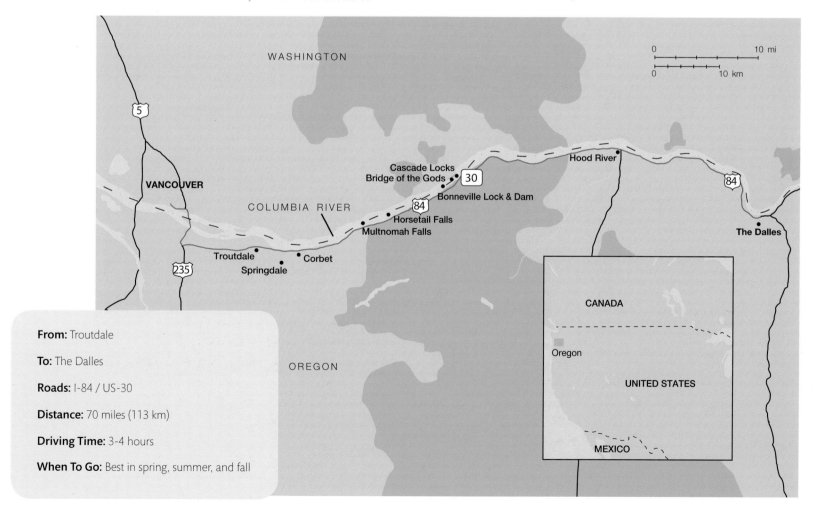

From: Troutdale

To: The Dalles

Roads: I-84 / US-30

Distance: 70 miles (113 km)

Driving Time: 3-4 hours

When To Go: Best in spring, summer, and fall

pass the Cascades Rapids and venture upriver as far as The Dalles. From May to October, a sternwheeler river boat runs river cruises from here. Again, this is a highly recommended diversion from the road. From the deck, visitors can enjoy amazing river and gorge views and watch Native American tribes fishing.

A little further upriver is the lively town of Hood River, full of restaurants and shops. Close by is the Historic Columbia River Highway State Trail, which incorporates stretches of the original Columbia River Byway that fell out of use after the Bonneville Dam was opened in 1936 and the new "water grade route" (I-84) was built in the 1950s. Now restored, more than 12 miles (19 km) of the old highway have been re-opened for hikers and cyclists. Other sections of the old road can also be accessed at the Tooth Rock Trailhead, which offers great views of the Bonneville Dam, as well as at the Bridge of the Gods Trailhead, which runs between the Tooth Rock Trailhead and Cascade Locks.

The route ends in The Dalles, where travelers wishing to learn more about the history of this fascinating and truly beautiful river road will find both the Columbia Gorge Discovery Center and Museum.

Right: The Rowena Loop, between Hood River and The Dalles near the town of Rowena, is one of the most photographed stretches of road in Oregon.

Left: The Multnomah Falls is one of the USA's tallest, at 620 feet (189 m).

MUST SEE

Road-trippers should definitely break their journey at the **Portland Women's Forum Scenic Viewpoint** and the **Vista House** for wonderful views of the **Columbia River** and **gorge**. Of the river's many waterfalls the **Wahkeena Falls** and **Multnomah Falls** (one of the USA's biggest cascades) are especially lovely.

Also well worth a visit are the **Bonneville Lock and Dam National Historic Landmark**, the **Bridge of the Gods**, and **Cascade Locks** where you can leave the car and take a river cruise. Hikers and cyclists will also enjoy taking in sections of the **Historic Columbia River Highway State Trail** before finishing the route at **The Dalles**.

LAS VEGAS TO DEATH VALLEY
NEVADA

Funeral Mountains, Starvation Canyon, Deadman Pass, and Coffin Peak. They are all to be found in Death Valley, and provide a hint of the tough history of this barren and foreboding valley east of the Sierra Nevada Mountains. But at the same time this long, slender valley – it's about 130 miles (209 km) long and just 12 miles (19.3 km) wide – is a place of almost exquisite beauty with brightly colored rock formations, untouched sand dunes, and unworldly salt flats.

DEATH VALLEY IS ALSO 282 FEET (86 M) BELOW SEA LEVEL AT ITS LOWEST AND THIS PARTLY EXPLAINS WHY THIS AREA GETS SO SERIOUSLY HOT – temperatures often go higher than 130°F (55°C) in summer – so it's probably best visited in late fall or winter time. This route takes you to some of Death Valley's most famous attractions and though it could – just – be done in a day, an

overnight stay and two days would be preferable. Starting from Las Vegas, take the I-95 past Red Rock Canyon National Park, part of the Mojave Desert. Then at Amargosa Valley turn left onto Highway 373, cross the State Line into California and shortly after turn right onto CA 190. The Funeral Mountains Wilderness Area and Bat Mountain are on your right. Look for the left turn into Furnace Creek Road then turn

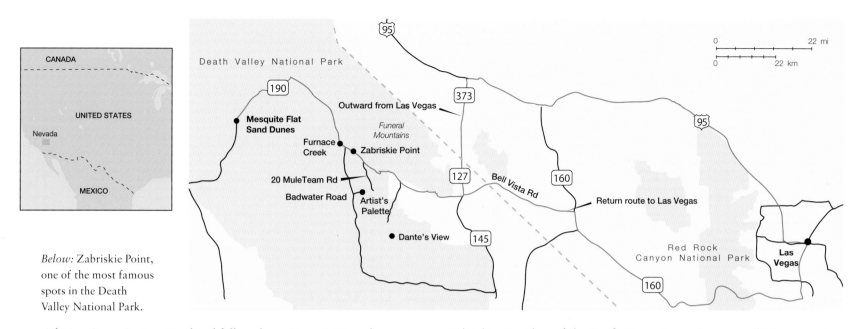

Below: Zabriskie Point, one of the most famous spots in the Death Valley National Park.

right into Dante's View Road and follow this to Dante's View close to the Black Mountains, from where there are wonderful views of much of the southern part of Death Valley. From the car park you can walk to the top of Dante's Peak for even better views, or take a longer hike to Coffin Peak for alternative vistas.

Now retrace the 13 miles (21 km) to CA 190, turn left, then after 7 miles (11 km) turn left to Zabriskie Point, named after Christian Zabriskie, President of the Pacific Coast Borax Company which operated here in the early 20th century, and made famous by Michelangelo Antonioni's 1970 movie of the same name. Now, it's one of Death Valley's most famous places, thanks to the extraordinarily eroded and colored rock formation all around. The views are amazing at any time but are truly spectacular at sunrise and sunset as the low yellow sunlight creates entirely new panoramas.

From Zabriskie Point it's just a few miles along CA 190 to Furnace Creek, one of the few towns in Death Valley where you will find hotels, stores, a fuel station, and even a golf course.

From Furnace Creek it's 22 miles (35 km) along CA 190 to Salt Creek. It's usually dry but a little brackish water remains in some areas and bizarrely this is inhabited by Pupfish, the last remaining fish from what before the Ice Age was Lake Manly, which subsequently dried up leaving today's Death Valley.

Ten minutes' drive further along CA 190 is the Devil's Cornfield with its strange Arroweed plants, then 3.7 miles (6 km) further take a right turn to the Mesquite Flat Sand Dunes, used to film many movie desert scenes including Star Wars.

Now retrace your steps back to Furnace Creek, then turn right into Badwater Road which takes you to the Badwater Basin, the lowest point in North America at 282 feet (86 m) below sea level.

Return some 10 miles (16 km) along Badwater Road then turn right into Artist's Drive which rises up a deep canyon in the Black Mountains

Top: Dante's View, from where much of the southern part of Death Valley can be seen.

Above: The Mesquite Flat Sand Dunes and, in the distance, the foothills of the Amargosa Range. This arid landscape is where many movies, including some of the *Star Wars* franchise, were filmed.

MUST SEE

Death Valley has numerous famous visitor sites including **Dante's View, Zabriskie Point**, the **Mesquite Flat Sand Dunes**, the **Badwater Basin**, and the **Twenty Mule Team Road.**

The **Furnace Creek Visitor Center and Museum** provides information and sets the historical scene.

to Artist's Palette – multi-colored rock formations created by the slow oxidization of iron salts, mica, and manganese – it's at its best in late afternoon light.

From here return to Badwater Road and drive some 9 miles (15 km) to Golden Canyon where parts of early *Star Wars* movies were filmed. There's a 2 mile (3.2 km) hike through the golden canyons and boulders to the Red Cathedral geological formation at the end.

Now follow Badwater Road back to the junction with CA 190 and turn right. After 4 miles (6.45 km) you will come to the Twenty Mule Team Road. It's an unpaved 2.7 mile (4.4 km) one-way loop road but perfectly accessible for ordinary cars. Named after the mule trains that pulled borax from the Death Valley mines in the late 19th century, the trail passes old mines, canyons, narrow ravines, and contrasting colored badlands.

Return to CA 190 and follow the road to Death Valley Junction, then cross the state line into Nevada and turn right into Bel Vista Road which joins Highway 160 which takes you back to Las Vegas.

Above: The glitz, lights, and the glamor of Las Vegas make this desert city the perfect starting point for trips to Death Valley or the nearby Grand Canyon.

Following pages: The Badwater Basin, the lowest point in continental USA at 282 feet (86 m) below sea level, where the salty deposits are clearly visible.

From: Las Vegas

To: Death Valley

Roads: I-95, Highway 373, CA 190, Bell Vista Road, Highway 160

Distance: 390 miles (626 km)

Driving Time: 8.5 hours

When To Go: Best fall and winter

GOING-TO-THE-SUN ROAD
MONTANA

Going-to-the-Sun Road was constructed in Montana's Glacier National Park in 1932 to encourage motorists to visit the park and enjoy its 1,583 square miles (4,099 km²) of mountains, lakes, rivers, and wilderness. In fact, this protected wilderness area is even larger as the park adjoins Canada's Waterton National Park, adding another 195 square miles (505 km²) to be explored.

Below: St. Mary Lake with Wild Goose Island dwarfed by the size of the lake and the mountains surrounding it.

AT JUST 50 MILES (80.5 KM) IN LENGTH, THE ROUTE OFFERS A RELATIVELY SHORT JOURNEY – it could be covered in around two hours – but travelers should allow much more time than this. Firstly, because there is a speed limit of 45 mph (72 km/h) on the lower sections and just 25 mph (40 km/h) on the higher Alpine section. Secondly, because they will want to stop often in order to appreciate some of the USA's finest scenery. It is also important to note that large vehicles are prohibited and there are no gas stations along the route, so make sure you fill up first. In high season it is a good idea to start the drive early. The most popular parking areas – including those at Logan Pass – can get very busy.

Starting in the west, Going-to-the-Sun Road begins next to the West Glacier Amtrak railroad station where it leaves Route 2. The main park entrance is a mile further along the road and after another mile you will arrive at the Apgar Visitor Center, where park rangers are available to answer questions. Very soon after, travelers will catch their first glimpse of Lake McDonald, a 10 mile (16 km) expanse that offers wonderful vistas. Those with time to spare can rent a canoe and paddleboard here, or take one of the lake cruises from various points along the shore.

Most people stop at the McDonald Falls at Mile 12. A relatively easy hiking path from the road takes in both the falls and the Sacred Dancing Cascade. A little further along the road, at Mile 16, there's an even easier hiking trail through forests where visitors can see western red cedars, black cottonwoods, and western hemlocks. These magnificent trees – some of which are over 500 years old – are usually only found in the Pacific Northwest.

Continue through the West Side Tunnel to The Loop Switchback at Mile 24. Here, the road turns back on itself in a tight hairpin bend (one of the major reasons larger vehicles are banned). A parking area at The

Above: The West and East Side tunnels were hacked out entirely by hand as no power tools were available in such a remote spot.

Loop provides great views of Heavens Peak, a permanently snow-covered mountain that rises 8,987 feet (2,740 m), and also marks the entrance to the Loop Trail which offers yet more stunning views of the scenery.

There are more than 200 waterfalls in the Glacier National Park. Another to see from this road is Bird Woman Falls at Mile 27, a 500 foot (152 m) marvel that is particularly spectacular in spring and early summer when the deluge is swollen by melt water from the mountains and glacier. Later in the year, it's often dry. If so, visitors might be luckier at the smaller Haystack Falls a mile further along the road.

At Mile 32 the road reaches its highest point, Logan Pass, at 6,646 feet (2,205 m). Expect fabulous 360 degree panoramic views from the visitor center, or take one of the hiking trails – to Hidden Lake or the Highline Trail – for different views and the chance to spot mountain wildlife. Mountain goats and bighorn sheep are often seen here. Elk and even grizzly bears might also be around.

As mentioned earlier, Going-to-the-Sun Road represents an astonishing feat of engineering and a clear demonstration of this can be found at the East Side Tunnel. Here, the rock was entirely hacked out by hand as no power machinery was available in such a remote spot during the early 20th century.

The best view of the Jackson Glacier can be found at the parking area at Mile 37. Look south for the 10,052 foot (3,062 m) Mount Jackson, the fourth-highest mountain in the park. There is no missing the glacier even though it's considerably smaller now than in the past.

As travelers come to the last stage of their journey they will arrive at Wild Goose Island at Mile 43. It's well worth making another stop here. In the middle of St. Mary Lake, the island is a popular site for photography and there is plenty of opportunity for more sightseeing, hiking, and boating. Going-to-the-Sun Road ends soon after, at the town of St. Mary.

Left: Bird Woman Falls plummets dramatically down the mountainside and right underneath the road.

Far right: Lake McDonald, the largest lake in Montana's Glacier National Park. The road runs along its southern shore.

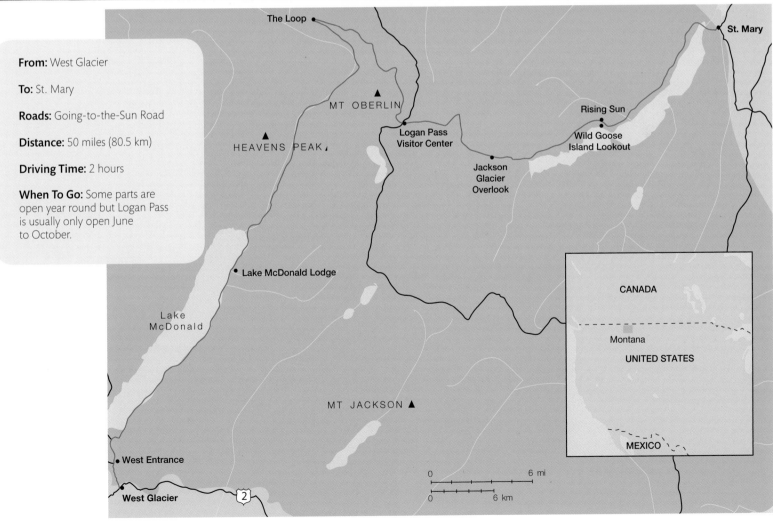

From: West Glacier

To: St. Mary

Roads: Going-to-the-Sun Road

Distance: 50 miles (80.5 km)

Driving Time: 2 hours

When To Go: Some parts are open year round but Logan Pass is usually only open June to October.

The Loop

St. Mary

MT OBERLIN

Rising Sun

Logan Pass
Visitor Center

Wild Goose
Island Lookout

HEAVENS PEAK

Jackson
Glacier
Overlook

Lake McDonald Lodge

CANADA

Lake
McDonald

Montana

UNITED STATES

MT JACKSON

MEXICO

West Entrance

0   6 mi

West Glacier

0   6 km

UTAH SCENIC BYWAY 12
UTAH

The 124-mile (199 km) Utah Scenic Byway 12 can easily be driven in two to three hours but, as with so many of the drives in this book, most people prefer to linger on the route – two to three days is ideal – taking in the sheer variety of communities, landscapes, history, and culture that this extraordinary road has to offer. Indeed, Scenic Byway 12 is also designated as an "All-American Road", thanks to the unique places road-trippers encounter along the way – the massive Dixie National Forest, two national parks, a recently-designated national monument, and three further state parks.

THE ROUTE STARTS IN THE EAST, SEVEN MILES (11.2 KM) SOUTH OF THE TOWN OF PANGUITCH AT THE JUNCTION WITH US HIGHWAY 89. Before setting off it is worth visiting Panguitch itself: it's a town brimming with historic landmarks and reminders of its early Mormon settlers. After beginning the drive,

travelers will very soon see the terracotta red, orange, and rust colors of the Red Canyon's rocks over the forest canopy below. The road then passes through the two red-rock stone arches that mark the unofficial gateway to Bryce Canyon National Park. Though the road journey has only just begun, most people make an early stop to explore the park,

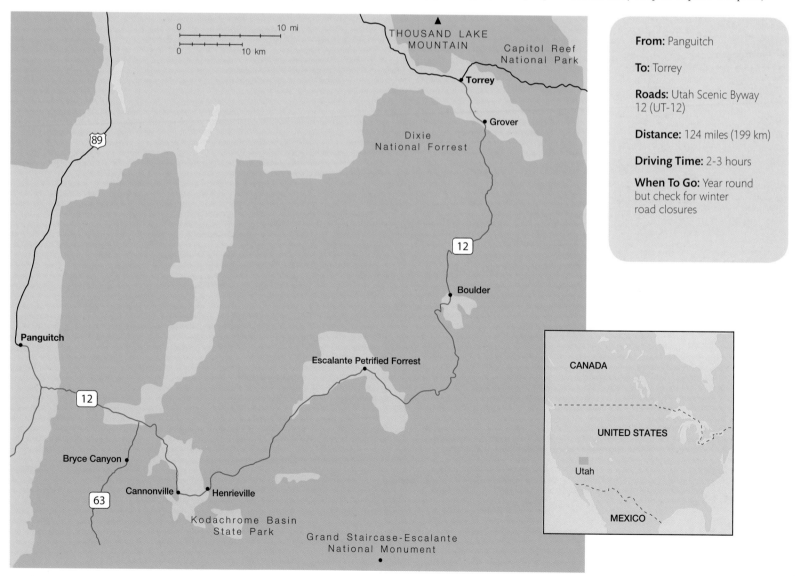

From: Panguitch

To: Torrey

Roads: Utah Scenic Byway 12 (UT-12)

Distance: 124 miles (199 km)

Driving Time: 2-3 hours

When To Go: Year round but check for winter road closures

Above: The well-preserved town of Panguitch was first settled by Mormon pioneers in 1864. Its name derives from the Paiute Indian word meaning "Big Fish".

Left: Red Canyon in Bryce National Park, where sandstone is a dominant geological feature.

Below: One of the outstanding views along Highway 12 is the Grand Staircase–Escalante Monument.

Above: Sunset Point in Bryce Canyon National Park, a landscape created by millions of years of erosion.

MUST SEE

This route winds through some of the United States' most rugged landscape, where pink and russet stone has been carved into canyons and stone pillars, and the sights it offers are simply astounding.

Don't miss the **Red Canyon** and its stone archways, **Bryce Canyon National Park**, **Kodachrome Basin National Park**, **Escalante Petrified Forest State Park**, the amazing **Hogsback** section of road, **Capital Reef National Park**, the **Anasazi State Park Museum**, or the **Grand Staircase–Escalante National Monument**.

which boasts the world's largest number of hoodoos – strangely shaped rocks left standing after millions of years of erosion. To see the wonders of Bryce Canyon – including the Amphitheatre, Rainbow Point, Sunset Point, Sunrise Point, and Inspiration Point, all of which offer stunning views over a truly unique landscape – take Highway 63 off UT-12, but be aware that this is a very popular excursion. It's best to visit early or late in the day if you want to miss the crowds.

At the town of Cannonville there is a tempting detour along Kodachrome Road and Cottonwool Canyon Road to the Kodachrome Basin National Park. Here, travelers will find themselves some 5,800 feet (1,768 m) above sea level among 67 monolithic stone spires, created by erosion over hundreds of millions of years. The colors of the rocks and their layers of sediment have to be seen to be believed, and are so vivid that the area was named for the well-known Kodak color transparency film in 1948.

Continuing along UT-12 for 15 miles (24 km), the next stop is Henrieville – a small town high on the plateau in Garfield County, overlooked by the dark red Escalante Mountains. Another short detour

takes drivers to the Escalante Petrified Forest State Park with its lava fields and areas of petrified wood.

The next stretch of road offers yet more amazing panoramas as it crosses the Hogsback, a raised section of road with steep drops – and incredible views of bizarre rock formations – on both sides. It leads into the town of Boulder, from where there is yet another possible 30 mile (48 km) detour into the Capital Reef National Park. Boulder is also home to the Anasazi State Park Museum where visitors can wander around an ancestral pueblo village dating back to around 1000 CE.

The next section of the route crosses the Dixie National Forest with its mighty aspen and pine trees, high up at an altitude of over 9,000 feet (2,743 m). At the road's highest point visitors will find an outlook from where the Henry Mountains, the Grand Staircase–Escalante National Monument, and the Capitol Reef National Park can be viewed. All of these are also worth a visit, but will take time. The Grand Staircase–Escalante National Monument alone is set in an area of 1.9 million acres (7,700 km₂), making it larger than the state of Delaware. An incredible vista of massive natural steps that descend toward the Grand Canyon

in Arizona, the site was designated a national monument by President Clinton in 1996. Home to abundant flora and fauna, it is one of the most impressive sights along a route that is hardly short of amazing views.

The small town of Grover, originally settled in 1880 and named for President Grover Cleveland, is another gateway to Capitol Reef National Park with its desert landscapes and sandstone cliffs. Again, a detour into the park will not be a short one. The major geological feature of the area is the 100-mile- (161-km-) long Waterpocket Fold, an area of the Earth's crust that over the millennia has been eroded into a magnificent series of canyons, enormous domes, and towering monoliths. Anyone choosing to explore here should look out for golden eagles, deer, racoons, and antelope. Bears, coyote, and mountain lions also live here and might be spotted by luckier visitors.

The eastern gateway to Scenic Byway 12 is the town of Torrey, settled by Mormon pioneers in 1880. Overlooked by Thousand Lake Mountain, it is a delightful, quiet, and pretty town with tree-lined roads, small shops, and a number of restaurants – the perfect place to end an amazing journey.

MONUMENT VALLEY
ARIZONA – UTAH

If Monument Valley looks familiar, it's because it features in countless movies and photographic shoots, including classic films such as Stagecoach, Forrest Gump, *and* Easy Rider. *What attracted movie directors and photographers is what makes this drive so special: miles of red-rock desert and strange sandstone outcrops at the very heart of the Navajo Native American culture.*

THE DRIVE THROUGH THE VALLEY – ON HIGHWAY 163 FROM KAYENTA, ARIZONA, IN THE SOUTH, TO MEXICAN HAT, UTAH, IN THE NORTH – covers only 43 miles (69 km), which would normally take not much more than an hour. However, the scenery here is so unusual and enchanting that it would be all but impossible to resist the temptation to stop along the way. Furthermore, there's a 17 mile (27 km) loop on unmade dirt roads that takes road-

trippers into the Navajo reserve. It costs $20 per car but would be foolish to miss. Cross the Arizona/Utah state line and you will soon see the well-signposted turn to the right along Monument Valley Road to the

Below: Monument Valley is most famous for its red sandstone outcrops that have been eroded and shaped by wind and rain over millions of years.

Monument Valley Navajo Tribal Visitor Center. If you plan to take the Valley Drive, make sure you have water and sufficient fuel: there are no facilities in the reserve. Any 4x4 and most standard cars will handle the dirt roads, but low-slung sports cars and RVs with long overhangs are not recommended. It's also worth checking the park website if there have been heavy rains – the roads can become impassable. Entry is from early morning to early evening for most of the year and either early or late is

From: Kayenta

To: Mexican Hat

Roads: Highway 163

Distance: 43 miles (69 km) plus 17 mile (27 km) loop

Driving Time: 5-6 hours

When To Go: Year Round but best in spring and fall

Above: A traditional Navajo home in Monument Valley. Called a *hogan*, it's a simple construction of wooden poles, tree bark, and mud. Traditionally the doorway always faced east to take advantage of the morning sun.

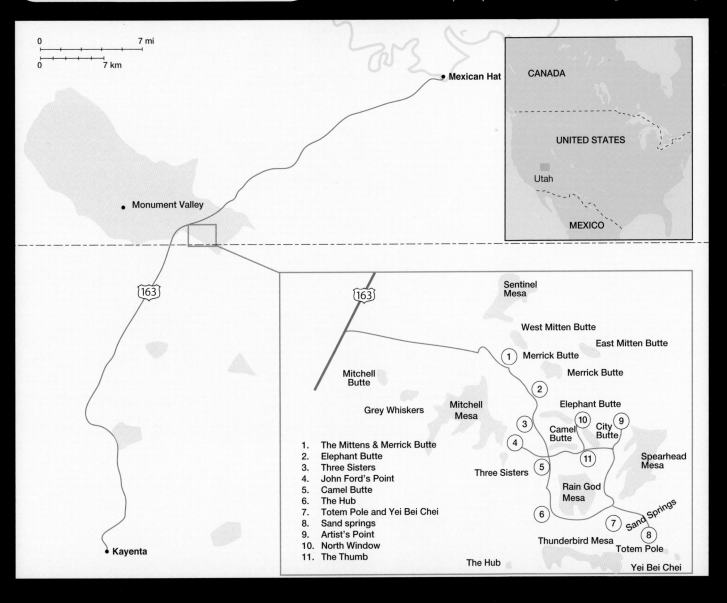

1. The Mittens & Merrick Butte
2. Elephant Butte
3. Three Sisters
4. John Ford's Point
5. Camel Butte
6. The Hub
7. Totem Pole and Yei Bei Chei
8. Sand springs
9. Artist's Point
10. North Window
11. The Thumb

Above: The West Mitten Butte, East Mitten Bute, and Merrick Butte at sunset in the Monument Valley Navajo Tribal Park.

Left: There's no mistaking the Mexican Hat outcrop.

MUST SEE

This is stunning desert country featuring amazing (and famous) rock formations so there's plenty to see along the route. A visit to the **Navajo Tribal Park** is a must. You can drive this part of the route alone, but are not permitted to leave the track unless hiring a local guide who can also tell you more about the culture and history of the Navajo tribe. The visitor center has a gift shop and café.

best for two reasons: less traffic and the light at this time of day makes for the finest views and vistas. In all, the track is 17 miles (27 km) in length, of which 13 (21 km) are a one-way loop. Expect to take between two to four hours because there's a 15 mph speed limit and the roads are bumpy and potholed in places. Visitors to the reserve must stay close to the track and may only venture further inland if accompanied by an official Navajo guide.

The first descent from the visitor center is the trickiest part of the drive but once completed, travelers soon reach the first of the most famous rock formations: the West Mitten Butte, the Merrick Butte, and the East Mitten Butte. On the right is the 1,000 foot (305 m) face of the Mitchell Mesa, which towers above the desert.

Next is the dark red, sheer-sided, Elephant Butte and then the Three Sisters – slender pinnacles at the edge of the Mitchell Mesa that have

stunning locations along the way (all of which are well signposted) include John Ford's Point, named after the famous Hollywood director who used this location for a number of his Westerns; Camel Butte, the Rain God Mesa, and The Hub. The last is a lone spire surrounded by a small Navajo village.

Further along, the road arrives at Artist's Point and the North Window – one of the most popular stops along the route. Finally, look out for The Thumb, a rounded outcrop that (unlike Elephant Butte, which looks nothing like an elephant) does actually look like a thumb. From here the dirt road turns back to the visitor center and, from there, back to Highway 163. Turn right and drive to the end of Monument Valley at Mexican Hat, named for a rock formation that looks like an upside-down sombrero. Look out for the historic suspension bridge that takes the highway over the San Juan River before the junction with Utah

San Juan Skyway and the Million Dollar Highway
COLORADO

The San Juan Skyway is a 232 mile (373.5 km) loop through the San Juan Mountains in Colorado. Climbing to over 11,000 ft. (3,353 m) it passes through four national wilderness areas encompassing forests, flower meadows, rivers, waterfalls, historic mining towns, ancient Native-American ruins, expansive cattle ranges, and offers the very real chance of seeing black bears, bighorn sheep, mountain goats, elk, and deer.

AS THIS IS A LOOP, DRIVERS CAN START AND FINISH WHEREVER IS MOST CONVENIENT AND THE TOTAL JOURNEY WILL TAKE BETWEEN SIX AND SEVEN HOURS. But there is so much variety on the drive that anyone will want to take a great deal longer over what is one of America's most scenic drives.

If starting from Ridgway, take the US 550, and perhaps make a first stop very soon: at Ridgway State Park. With its fabulous views of the San Juan Mountains it is little wonder that this area is often called

Above: The Ridgeway State Park is also known as the "Switzerland of America" where it is overlooked by the snow-capped San Juan Mountains.

the "Switzerland of America". Along with the views, opportunities for hiking, fishing, boating, and even gold panning, can be found here.

From here drivers will be following the Uncompahgre River into the Uncompahgre National Forest and onto the town of Ouray, where the Million Dollar Highway starts. Ouray also boasts natural hot springs,

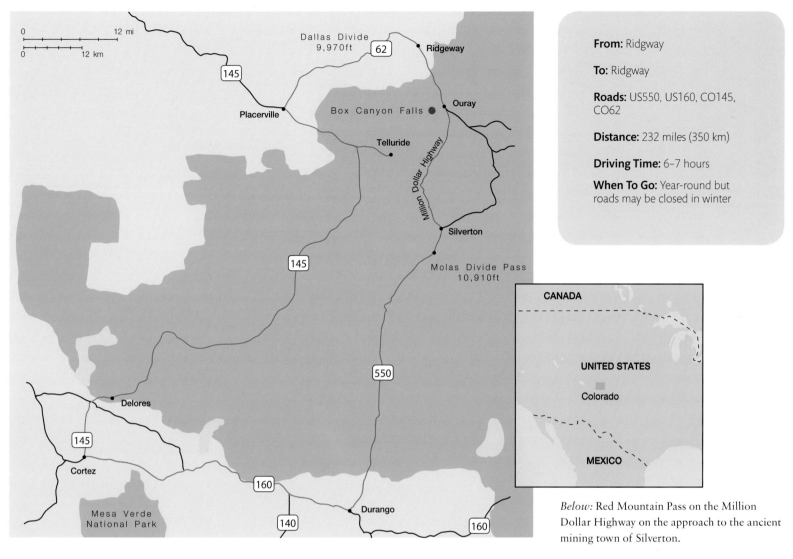

From: Ridgway

To: Ridgway

Roads: US550, US160, CO145, CO62

Distance: 232 miles (350 km)

Driving Time: 6–7 hours

When To Go: Year-round but roads may be closed in winter

Below: Red Mountain Pass on the Million Dollar Highway on the approach to the ancient mining town of Silverton.

and, before joining US 550, it's worth taking the short detour to Box Canyon Fall Park. Don't miss the Clear Creek Waterfall which plummets 285 feet (87 m) through a narrow gorge, best seen from the suspension bridge a short walk from the car parking area.

The first part of the Million Dollar Highway was built by Otto Mears in 1883 as a toll road between Ouray and Ironton. Later, a second toll road was constructed to connect Ironton to Silverton, over the top of Red Mountain Pass. The whole route was reconstructed in 1924 and became US 550 when the original Federal Highway System was inaugurated in 1926. How this 25-mile (40 km) stretch received its name is uncertain. Some say it was because of the cost of constructing the road, while others believe it took the name from the value of gold and silver ore that was extracted from the thousands of tons of materials dug out to create the road. It's also possible that it derives from the dreams of wealth of those who trekked here in search of fortunes. What is certain is that this rugged stretch of the San Juan Mountains contained vast quantities of gold and silver, which is why there are so many old and abandoned mines along the route.

The roads are kept open year round but in winter it's best to check the conditions with the Colorado Department of Transportation before setting out.

MUST SEE

Don't miss **Ridgway State Park** – the "Switzerland of America", nor the **Ouray hot springs** and **Clear Creek Waterfall**. The **Million Dollar Highway** is a lasting testament to the blood, sweat and toil of the old silver and gold miners, as is the old mining town of **Silverton**.

The **Mesa Verde National Park** with its cliff houses, is an extraordinary sight and the **Chapin Mesa Archaeological Museum** provides all you need to know about the prehistoric civilizations of this mountainous region.

Far right: Once an important mining town, Durango is now a magnet for hikers, campers, horseriders, rock climbers, fishermen and rafters, and kayakers.

Below: Expect dramatic scenery on the Million Dollar Highway as US 550 rises into the San Juan mountains.

The weather can change very rapidly at these heights and in winter heavy snowfalls, landslides, and avalanches are regular occurrences.

The first section of the Million Dollar Highway winds along the valley of the Uncompahgre River and, later, Red Mountain Creek. The Uncompahgre Gorge is the first of many stunning sights. Here, the road that is carved from the side of the mountain – often with no guard rails – and passes over near-vertical cliff tops with the raging river far below.

Next, the US 550 heads up into the mountains past Ironton. Look out for numerous old mines along the way, including the remains of the long-abandoned Idarado Mine – an old gold mine that can be seen from the road. After this road trippers will be heading up the Red Mountain Pass toward Red Mountain Town. Enjoy magnificent views of mountains, gullies and gorges, rivers and waterfalls as the road reaches 11,018 feet (3,358 m) at the summit of Red Mountain Pass, where the San Juan National Forest starts.

This US National Forest, established in 1905, offers 1,878,46 acres (760 km²) of wilderness areas, scenic byways, and historic sights including old gold mining ghost towns and ancient Puebloan cliff dwellings and pit houses. The Puebloan people lived mainly in the American southwest between AD 750 and 1300, but some ventured as far

north as Colorado and Utah. Red Mountain, which takes its name from the oxidized minerals at its surface, is actually a collapsed volcano cone. Back in 1860, the hardened ancient lava flows were found to contain gold – enough for an estimated $750 million worth to be mined here over the following 30 years or so, from colorfully-named mines such as Yankee Girl, National Belle, Cora Belle, and Joke Tunnel.

After Red Mountain, the Million Dollar Highway winds downward toward Silverton. This former silver mining camp also boasted some gold mines and today the Old Hundred Gold Mine Tour provides not just a comprehensive history of gold mining in the area, but also offers visitors the chance to pan for gold. Silverton itself retains many of the Victorian-style buildings erected during its heyday in the late 1800s and more than 50 historic buildings can be seen on a tour of the town, including a museum in the old County Jail building. Silverton is also the northern terminus of the famous Durango to Silverton Narrow Gauge Railroad which runs for some 45 miles (72 km) along tracks originally laid to transport silver and gold ore from the mountains to Durango – a railroad first built in 1881.

Keep on the US 550 up to the Molas Pass. Over the next few miles travelers pass Molas Lake, Andrews Lake, and Haviland Lake, all of which offer spectacular mountain views, fishing, hiking, and camping. Continue to the town of Durango, once an important commercial hub. Worth a visit are the Strater Hotel, formerly frequented by the railroad barons, the Denver and Rio Grande Railroad Depot, and numerous colonial-era houses that were built in a range of styles. Durango also marks the start of the Colorado Trail, which stretches from here to Denver, 469 miles (755 km) away. Here, the scenery starts to change, too: to high desert. Road trippers can expect to see cacti in the coming miles.

The road now turns west on the US 160. Pass the Mesa Verde National Park, famous for its cliff houses constructed by the Anasazi tribe more than 1500 years ago. The park boasts thousands of prehistoric archaeological sites and the Chapin Mesa Archaeological Museum where visitors can learn more about the area's fascinating past.

Keep on the US 160 to Cortez, then turn onto the CO 145 to Delores before following the Delores River through Rico. Just after, is the astonishing volcanic Lizard Head Peak. Head on down the pass to Trout Lake, after which the road descends steeply into the valleys. Some 10 miles (16 km) further on there is an intersection signpost pointing the way to the ski resort of Telluride. It's worth a detour to see the first bank robbed by Butch Cassidy back in 1898, as well as Colorado's longest waterfall – the Bridal Veil Falls – and the town's numerous museums and art galleries.

Continue, following the San Miguel River on the CO 145 then join the CO 62 near Placerville. The road takes drivers up again over the Dallas Divide Mountain at 8,970 ft. (2,734 m) before descending into Ridgeway where the journey started and now ends.

Above: Silverton station at the start of the famous 45 miles (72 km) Silverton to Durango Narrow Gauge Railroad.

Left: The Yankee Girl mine is one of many old gold and silver mines to be found along the route. Opened in 1882, Yankee Girl was one of the most profitable mines of them all and produced silver, copper, and gold.

Far left: Ouray, with its natural hot springs, has been welcoming travelers for more than 100 years. Many of the original Victorian buildings have been restored and are still occupied, adding to the town's old world charm.

Following pages: Some 600 ancient cliff houses are still preserved in the Mesa Valley National Park. They were first built by the Anasazi tribe around 1,500 years ago.

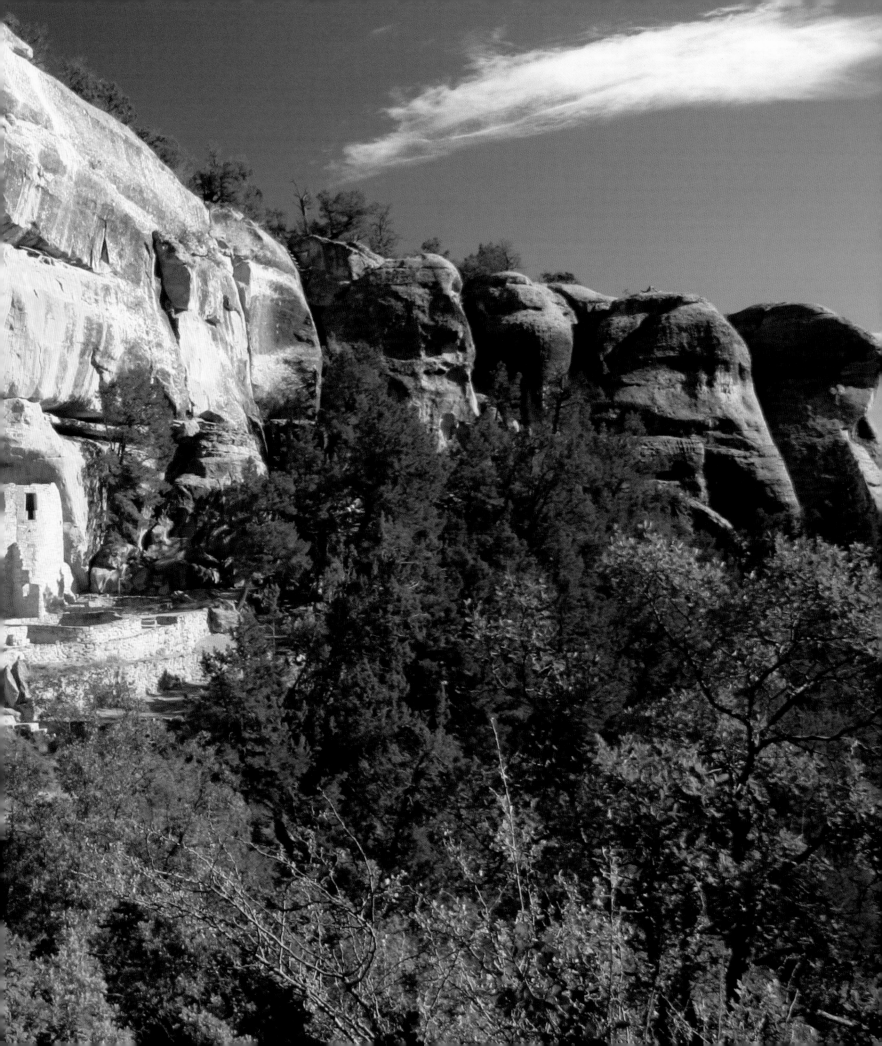

PIKES PEAK HIGHWAY
COLORADO

The first track to reach the top of Pikes Peak was completed in 1888 and advertised by the Cascade and Pikes Peak Toll Road Company as "the highest in the world". By 1915, a full road had been completed and, just a year later in 1916, the first Pikes Peak International Hill Climb was held, making it the USA's second oldest motor sport event. That first "Race to the Clouds" involved 39 cars with the winner, Rea Lentz, reaching the top in a little under 21 minutes to lift the $1,000 first prize. As of today, the record is held by Sebastian Loeb who set a time of 8 minutes, 13.8 seconds in 2013, driving a specially prepared 875 bhp Peugeot Rally Car.

THOUGH IT'S THE ANNUAL PIKES PEAK RACE THAT GIVES THE MOUNTAIN ITS INTERNATIONAL FAME, for the rest of the year this highway offers a gentle, beautiful, and beguiling drive along which the road bends and curves from the start – already at 7,400 feet (2,255 m) above sea level – to its summit at 14,110 feet (4,300 m). Starting off Highway 24, a short drive from Colorado Springs, the Pikes Peak Highway passes the North Pole amusement park, after which drivers will arrive at toll booths where the cost is $15 for adults, $5 for children, or $50 per car. From here, the road starts climbing quite steeply through the Montane life zone at some 8,000 feet (2,400 m), before reaching Camera Point where travelers might wish to take advantage of the panoramic views over the Ute Pass and the City of Cascade. Don't miss the famous Big Foot crossing sign, shortly after the Mile 3 marker, where a Big Foot was allegedly seen in 2001. Continue through aspen woodland to Crystal

Creek Reservoir, which comes up at Mile 6. Cross the dam at the end of the reservoir, where a visitor center offers amazing views, especially in the fall when the trees change color to vibrant red, yellow, and orange.

Not far beyond the visitor center is the start point of the famous hill climb. Here, the road begins to climb more steeply. Between Mile 7 and 8 travelers can take their cameras out again for the Peak View Photo Stop, which has great views of the distant peak. Between Mile 9 and 10 is a large picnic stop after which you will enter the Sub-Alpine life zone before finding the former Glen Cove Ski Area between Mile 11 and 12, though the old ski slopes have been replanted. Continue into the Alpine

Left: Crystal Creek Reservoir, overlooked by Pikes Peak.

Right: Expect the unexpected. A Big Foot was allegedly seen in 2001 on the road up to Pikes Peak.

From: Gateway off Highway 24

To: Summit of Pikes Peak

Roads: Pikes Peak Highway

Distance: 19 miles (30.5 km)

Driving Time: 2-3 hours round trip

When To Go: Open year round but check weather in wintertime

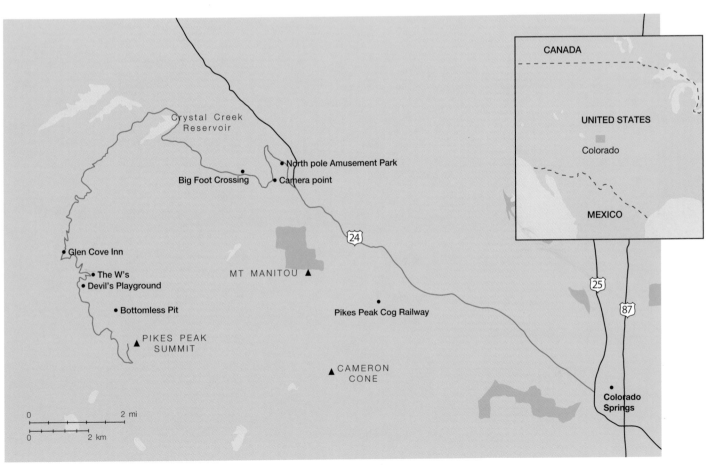

Above: Amazing views from the 14,110 feet (4,300 m) scenic stop on the Pikes Peak Highway.

Far right: The Garden of the Gods Park in Colorado Springs with Pikes Peak in the distance.

Following pages: One of the many hairpin bends on the road to the summit of Pikes Peak.

MUST SEE

This is a stunning journey through the Colorado landscape. Along the way, keep a look out for elk, deer, marmots, and Rocky Mountain bighorn sheep as well as amazing views. Stop at **Big Foot** crossing and maybe spend a little time watching for rare wildlife.

The **Crystal Reservoir Visitor Center**, **Halfway Picnic Grounds**, **Glen Cove**, and the **Devil's Playground** are all fine stopping places, too.

In addition, there are smaller parking areas all along the route, each offering its own unique views. As you pass the start point of the **Pikes Peak International Hill Climb**, imagine what it must be like attaining speeds of over 100 mph (160 km/h) during the annual race to the top! For everyone else, the speed limit is 25 mph.

zone to the Glen Cove Inn, with its restaurant, gift shop, and restrooms. (On the return trip down the mountain, you may well be stopped here by rangers checking brake temperatures.)

From the inn to the summit, the views change radically, particularly after leaving the tree line behind at around Mile 14. Now you will reach the "Ws" – a series of bends that, when viewed from above, look like … a W. The first is at Mile 14.5. The second is even more dramatic. In recent years guard rails have been installed, but before this it was not a good area for those with vertigo.

At Mile 16 travelers arrive at the Devils' Playground, an area prone to dramatic lightning storms. Stop here for great views of the "Ws" and beyond. Shortly after, at Mile 17, there is a parking area that no-one should miss. This is the Bottomless Pit, at the top of an immense drop. From here there are views of the distant Sangre de Cristo Mountain Range and the remains of the Ghost Town Hollow Mine some 1,500 feet (450 m) below.

At Mile 18 there is another parking area where tourists can often spot Rocky Mountain bighorn sheep. Soon after, the tracks of the Pikes Peak Cog Railway can be seen. An 8.9 mile (14.3 km) railway that was opened in 2007, it carries people to the summit during clement weather. At the summit itself there is plenty of parking, a weather station, the Summit House, and an observation deck boasting outstanding views in all directions – to Colorado Springs, the Rampart Range, the ghost town of Crystal, the Abyss of Desolation, and The Crater.

From here, visitors will descend again. The downward drive is, however, no anti-climax. New views and the vistas provide a completely different perspective of one of the USA's most momentous drives.

TURQUOISE TRAIL
NEW MEXICO

Not far outside the city of Albuquerque in New Mexico's high desert hills is the town of Tijeras. (If you are traveling from Albuquerque to Tijeras on Route 333, don't miss the "Musical Highway" along part of old Route 66. It's a stretch of road with rumble strips which, if you travel at exactly 45 mph (72 km/h), play the tune of "America the Beautiful".) Tijeras itself is the gateway to the Turquoise Trail – a 52 mile (84 km) National Scenic Byway through old mining and Gold Rush towns, many of which have been born again in modern times as vibrant and lively artists' communities.

THE ROUTE'S NAME DERIVES FROM THE BLUE TURQUOISE STONES THAT WERE HACKED FROM SHALLOW TRENCHES BY PUEBLOAN MINERS AS LONG AGO AS 900 CE. Then, the word the Native Americans used for turquoise was "chalichihuita", the "sky stone", and it was considered sacred. Later, gold, silver, lead, and coal were found in the region, attracting waves of settlers. Over the years many different communities grew up and died back here; their remnants can now be seen all along the trail.

Tijeras is located within the 1,633,783 acre (6,611.7 km²) Cibola National Forest and is the site of the famous Pueblo Ruin, an ancient pueblo dating to around 1300 CE that once had over 200 rooms, supporting a community of some 400 Native Americans. More of the history and culture of these ancient peoples can be found at the Museum of Archaeology and Material Culture in Cedar Crest, the next town you will come to as you follow this route through the ponderosa pine forest. Soon after, road-trippers will come to Sandia Park, a skiing area in the winter and a popular destination for hikers, horse-riders, and climbers

Above: San Francisco de Asis Church in Golden, one of the ghost towns along the Turquoise Trail.

Far left: Dramatic cloud formations over New Mexico.

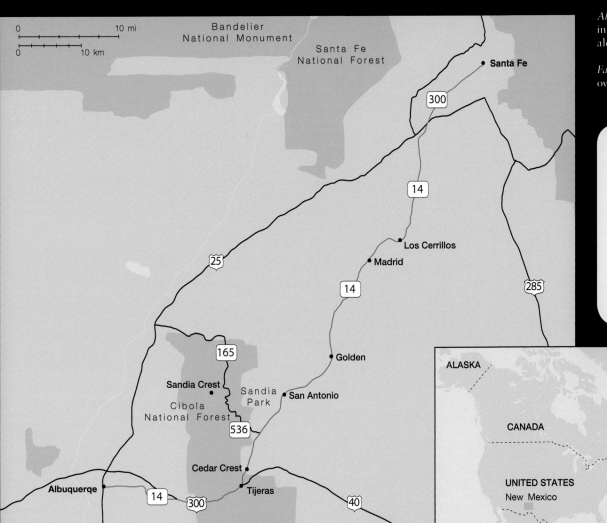

From: Tijeras

To: Santa Fe

Roads: NM-14

Distance: 52 miles (84 km)

Driving Time: 1-2 hours

When To Go: Year round

Above: The Oriz Mountains tower over the Turquoise Trail.

during the rest of the year. From here, travelers might wish to take a 13 miles (21 km) detour on NM 536 along the Sandia Crest Highway which journeys through the Cibola National Forest to the Sandia Peak Tramway, with its stunning views over Albuquerque, the Rio Grande Valley, and – on a clear day – all the way to Mount Taylor some 65 miles (104 km) distant. The Tinkertown Museum is also along this road and boasts an extraordinary collection of miniature figures and western and circus memorabilia put together by the folk artist Ross Ward.

Back on the Turquoise Trail, the road winds through sparse desert dotted with the occasional pine or juniper tree to the first ghost town of the route: Golden. Gold was discovered here in 1825, starting a frantic gold rush – the first west of the Mississippi River and more than 20 years earlier than the more famous Californian gold rushes. Sadly, the bonanza did not last long and the once rowdy community soon dwindled. Today, Golden has a population of about 50 but it still boasts the San Francisco Catholic church, built back in 1830.

MUST SEE

This is a route that takes in desert, mountains, deep canyons, and ancient history as well as re-built mining and Gold Rush towns that date to the time of the Wild West. For ancient culture, don't miss the **Pueblo Ruin in Tijeras**, the **Museum of Archaeology and Material Culture** in Cedar Crest, or the **San Cristobal Pueblo** in the Galisteo Basin.

Gold Rush and ghost towns can be found at **Golden**, **Madrid**, and **Los Cerrillos**. Take the **Sandia Peak Tramway** in Sandia Park to the top of the 10,678 foot (3,254 m) **Sandia Crest** for 360 degree views over vast tracts of New Mexico.

Madrid, the next stop along the route, was once another ghost town. At the end of the 19th century there were numerous large coal mines here but by the 1950s the mines had been closed and almost all the former 3,000 residents moved elsewhere. The entire deserted town was offered for sale at a price of $250,000 but remained unsold for the next 20 years. Today, the revitalized town is full of small shops, boutiques, galleries, and restaurants but still boasts enough of the old west atmosphere to have been used in numerous Hollywood films.

Three miles further on is Los Cerrillos, on the edge of the Cerrillos Hills where the majority of the local turquoise stones were mined over thousands of years. This was another Gold Rush town in the 1870s, at which time the burgeoning community is said to have supported over 20 bars and five brothels. Now, it has developed into another, far more peaceful, artists' community but the adobe fronts of the buildings and the fine old church on Main Street remain as they were a hundred years ago.

Continuing north from Los Cerrillos, the road passes through the Galisteo Basin, another area popular with movie directors. On this section of the trip is the J.W. Eaves Movie Ranch where over 250 movies have been shot, including *Easy Rider* and *Young Guns II*. It's also an important region of early history, known to have been inhabited by Paleo Indians from around some 7500 BCE. Many of the old pueblo ruins in the basin can be visited, including the San Cristobal Pueblo which once housed up to 1,000 people.

The end of the Turquoise Trail arrives a little north of Lone Butte/San Marcos at Santa Fe, back on the old Route 66.

Above: Madrid was once a thriving coal-mining community but today it's yet another ghost town along the route.

Below: An unusual double rainbow arcs over Albuquerque and the Sandia Mountains.

Following pages: Sandia Aerial Peak Tramway runs to the top of the 10,678 foot (3,254 m) Sandia Crest and offers stunning views over the Rio Grande Valley.

Texas Hill Country
Texas

Some 100 million years ago the site of this route was at the bottom of the ocean. As epochs passed, the land slowly rose to become the Edwards Plateau. The western part of the plateau is relatively flat, but the more easterly region has eroded over the years to form a landscape of hills, canyons, and valleys; its forests, wildflowers, and lakes fed by springs and rivers. Today, this is known as Hill Country. Stretching some 200 miles (322 km), there are numerous places to explore. This route – a loop from Austin to New Braunfels near San Antonio – is just one possibility.

START IN AUSTIN, THE "LIVE MUSIC CAPITAL OF THE WORLD" AND PERHAPS VISIT THE BOB BULLOCK TEXAS STATE HISTORY MUSEUM TO LEARN MORE ABOUT TEXAN HERITAGE. And if visiting between March and November, don't miss the spectacle of 1.5 million bats emerging from their roost under the Congress Avenue Bridge. From Austin, take TX-290, which – after around 20 miles (32 km) – rises up onto the Edwards Plateau. Pass through Dripping Springs and on to Henley. Just after, there's a turn onto Road 3232 that leads to the Pedernales Falls State Park where visitors can

Above: Millions of Brazilian free-tailed bats emerge each evening from their roost under the Congress Avenue Bridge in Austin.

see the limestone edge of the Edwards Plateau over which the Pedernales River falls in a series of cascades.

Johnson City is where President Lyndon B. Johnson was brought up and in the national park named for him you can visit his homestead and the family farms. LBJ Ranch – the Texas White House – is 14 miles (22.5 km) away.

From: Austin

To: New Braunfels

Roads: TX-290, TX-16, TX-246

Distance: 206 miles (332 km)

Driving Time: 4-5 hours

When To Go: Year round but best in spring

Right: New Braunfels was established back in 1845 by German immigrants and is today a thriving music center.

Below: Enchanted Rock near Fredericksburg. The 425 feet (130 m) tall mound is thought to be a billion years old.

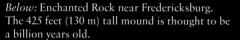

Another 30 miles (48 km) along TX-290 is the picturesque and historic old town of Fredericksburg. First settled by German immigrants, the town was strategically important during the Civil War. Numerous original timber and stone houses can still be found, particularly in the Historic District. A short 18 miles (29 km) detour north of Fredericksburg takes road-trippers to the Enchanted Rock State Natural Area, home to a massive pink granite rock dome some 425 feet (130 m) tall and thought to be a billion years old. It's possible to climb to the top, from where there are great views over an area sometimes called "the Heart of Texas".

From Fredericksburg, TX-16 follows the bends and meanderings of the Guadelupe River south toward Kerrville. Here, travelers might wish to leave the car to visit the Museum of Western Art and the Hill Country Museum, or hike, swim, and relax in the Kerrville-Schreiner State Park, which is in town on the banks of the river. Stay on the winding TX-16 to Bandera. This route is a little longer than the more direct TX-173 option, but worth taking as it reveals the beauty of Hill Country. This area is renowned for its wildflower displays – especially the bluebonnets in April. Bandera bills itself the "Cowboy Capital of the World" and is home to the Frontier Times Museum where tourists can learn about the

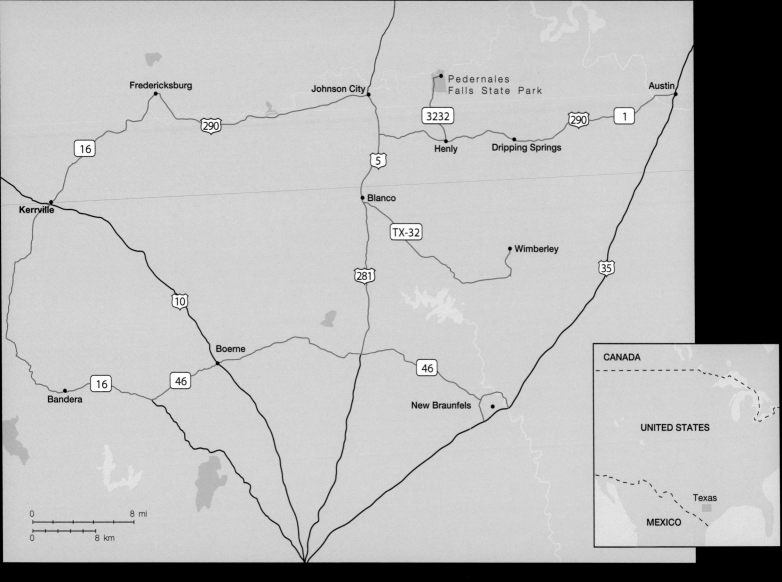

lawless frontier days. Restaurants, shops, and live country music ensure a lively welcome for visitors and this is also a good base for hiking, horse-riding, hunting, cycling, or visiting one of the local vineyards.

From Bandera stay on TX-16 south then look for the turn left onto TX-46. This takes road-trippers first to the town of Boerne – famous for its antique shops. After another 13 miles (21 km) on the same road there is a left turn toward the Guadalupe River State Park. This is also an excellent stopping point for folk who enjoy the great outdoors. Here, visitors can hike, swim, boat, and fish. Floating downriver on an inflated tube is also great fun.

A little further along the road there is an intersection with US-281. There's another detour opportunity here, northward to the Devil's Backbone – a limestone ridge running between Wimberley and Blanco and designated TX-32. Locals insist that the road is haunted but whether or not this is true it is one of the most scenic areas of the Texas Hill Country.

The rest of the journey to New Braunfels runs through gently rolling hills where the roadside is often lined by old oak and cedar trees. Once in New Braunfels – established back in 1845 by German immigrants – don't miss the Schlitterbahn Waterpark Resort, or a visit to Gruene. The latter is perfect for those seeking a more leisurely end to the journey. It is the oldest part of New Braunfels and home to Gruene Hall, which is famous for its country music and claims to be the oldest continuously open music hall in Texas.

MUST SEE

Austin's bats at nightfall, **Pedernales Falls State Park**, **Lyndon B. Johnson National Park**, **Fredericksburg**, **Enchanted Rock State Natural Area**, **Bandera** – the "Cowboy Capital of the World" – **the Devil's Backbone**, **New Braunfels**, and **Gruene**.

Right: Bluebonnets along the side of the road in Texas's Hill Country

LAKE SUPERIOR, MINNESOTA

Perhaps most famous for being name-checked in the title of Bob Dylan's 1965 album "Highway 61 Revisited", this route – especially its southern sections – is also known as "The Blues Highway". Dylan was a native of Duluth, Minnesota, and, back in his youth, Highway 61 stretched all the way south to New Orleans and was intimately connected with blues music. It passed close to the places where Charley Patton, Muddy Waters, and Elvis Presley were born. Bessie Smith was killed on Highway 61 in a car accident and Robert Johnson was reputed to have sold his soul to the devil along the road. This section of Highway 61 is at the northern end of the old route and covers a 145 mile (233 km) stretch along the north shore of Lake Superior, covering rugged country but offering unparalleled views over the waters of the great lake, cliff-faces, beaches, rivers, waterfalls, and thick forests.

THE ROUTE STARTS IN DULUTH, ON THE WESTERN SHORE OF LAKE SUPERIOR. The city is a major sea port. From here, shipping can access the open Atlantic Ocean – though only after an epic inland journey of over 2,300 miles (3,700 km) through the Great Lakes. In Duluth, it's almost impossible to miss the Aerial Lift Bridge, a massive structure built in 1905 that lifts vertically to allow ships to pass from Lake Superior into the protected waters of the twin ports of Duluth and Superior.

Once out of Duluth, Highway 61 quickly takes travelers to Two Harbors, some 27 miles (43.5 km) away, though some might prefer to take a detour along Old 61, Congdon Boulevard and Scenic Drive. This is a slower route but it runs closer to the shore and puts drivers closer to local businesses and restaurants.

In Two Harbors, a visit to the oldest lighthouse on Lake Superior, the Two Harbors Light, is recommended. Further on, after passing through the Silver Creek Cliff Tunnel, Gooseberry Falls State Park is also a popular visitor attraction, not least because of the scenic five waterfalls on the Gooseberry River. You can also see old lava flows at Agate Beach.

Second of the seven state parks along Highway 61 is Split Rock Lighthouse State Park, best known for the lighthouse from which it takes its name and which was built in 1910 atop a dramatic vertical cliff-face. Visitor tours are available from May to October but it's a great photo opportunity year-round.

After passing through the town of Silver Bay travelers arrive at Tettegouche State Park where an access road leads to Palisade Head, which has the highest cliffs in Minnesota, at 350 feet (106 m). On a clear day, this beautiful vantage point offers fabulous views of Lake Superior, right across to the Apostle Islands.

Above: Gooseberry Falls State Park is home to the Upper, Middle, and Lower Falls of the Gooseberry River.

Far left: The Aerial Lift Bridge at Duluth that lifts to allow ships access to the ports of Duluth and Superior.

Below: The Two Harbors Lighthouse is the oldest on Lake Superior.

Continue along Highway 61 past Little Marais. Here, the terrain becomes more mountainous. The route passes the ski resort of Lutsen in the Sawtooth Mountains, and the Cascade River State Park, before the road descends into Grand Marais. The town is well worth a visit for its picturesque port, downtown shopping, and historical area.

Approaching Grand Portage, and the end of the journey, travelers may wish to take another detour into the Grand Portage Indian Reservation before continuing into Grand Portage itself. An old fur trading town, and the site of an old Native American route to winter hunting grounds, Grand Portage received its name from French traders. In its heyday it was an important hub due to the impossibility of transporting goods through the local rivers because of the many rapids and waterfalls. Goods had to be carried from the interior to the shores of the lake. This trading post connected local trappers and hunters to the international trade routes. Today, the Grand Portage National Monument tells their fascinating story.

Another (non-driving) detour that is truly worth making is a boat trip from here to the Isle Royale National Park, open from April to October each year. A wholly unspoilt wilderness some 15 miles (24 km) to the east, and part of Michigan, this is the largest island on Lake Superior at 45 miles (72 km) long and 9 miles (14.5 km) wide. It offers hiking, sailing, kayaking, and scuba diving – but no driving as cars are banned.

MUST SEE

Watch the operation of the **Aerial Lift Bridge** in Duluth. Visit the lighthouses in **Two Harbors** and **Split Rock Lighthouse State Park**. **Palisade Head** offers amazing views over **Lake Superior**, while each of the seven state parks along the route provide stunning scenery of rivers, gorges, waterfalls, and beaches.

Grand Portage reveals what an old fur-trading town was really like, while **Isle Royale** offers true seclusion, abundant fauna and flora, and one of the region's last truly unspoilt wildernesses.

If everyone in the car has their passport with them, it is also possible to cross the Pigeon River from Grand Portage and continue over the border into Ontario, Canada, where Ontario Highway 61 continues to Thunder Bay a further 40 miles (64 km) north. You will have switched countries, and time zones, but the fabulous scenery remains exactly the same.

Right: Split Rock Lighthouse was built in 1910 on the top of cliffs overlooking Lake Superior.

Following pages: The Northern Lights reflected in the waters of Grand Portage.

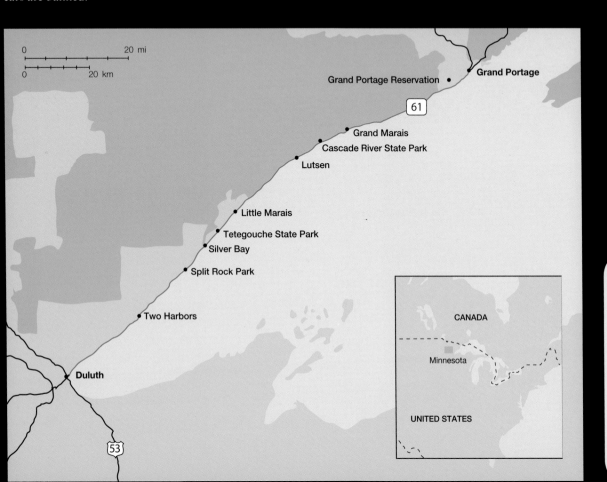

From: Duluth

To: Grand Portage

Roads: Highway 61

Distance: 145 miles (233 km)

Driving Time: 4 hours

When To Go: Open year round but check weather in wintertime

MISSISSIPPI GREAT RIVER ROAD I
MINNESOTA – MISSOURI

The 2,340 mile (3,765 km) Great River Road – which boasts of being the "Best Drive in America" – closely follows the mighty Mississippi River from Minnesota in the north to the Gulf of Mexico in the far south. Passing through ten states, it's the longest National Scenic Byway in the USA.

FROM START TO FINISH, THE GREAT RIVER ROAD (GRR) COULD BE COVERED IN AROUND 48 HOURS BUT MOST PEOPLE WOULD PLAN TO TAKE SEVERAL DAYS. Navigation is simple, because although it takes in a number of different federal, state, and local roads, the GRR – first developed in 1938 – is well signposted by a green steamboat inside a pilot's wheel.

Heading south, the GRR starts in Minnesota at Lake Itasca where the Mississippi has its source, passing through Grand Rapids, Minneapolis, St. Paul, and Winona before moving into Wisconsin. Each state looks after its own section of the GRR and maintains visitor centers and museums so it's worth spending some time checking out the best places to stop along the route and the attractions you most want to see.

In Minnesota the first section is serious fishing country but by the time you reach Grand Rapids, what started as a small brook and then became a reasonable sized river has already become a major industrial artery thanks to the thousands of lakes feeding into the upper reaches of the Mississippi.

Grand Rapids itself has a fine Itasca Heritage and Arts Center and upstairs a massive collection of Judy Garland memorabilia; the famous actress was born in the town and her former home is now the Judy Garland Museum.

Further on, the twin cities of Minneapolis and St. Paul have numerous visitor attractions including the famous Minneapolis Sculpture Garden and the Minnesota History Center.

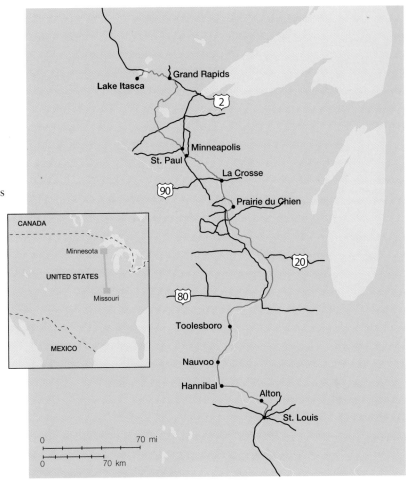

From: Lake Itasca

To: St. Louis

Roads: All signposted as one of America's National Scenic Byways

Distance: 1,472 miles (2,368 km)

Driving Time: 32 hours

When To Go: Year-round

Left: One of the attractions in the twin cities of St. Paul and Minneapolis is the Minneapolis Sculpture Garden, one of the largest sculpture gardens in the USA.

Far left: The Mississippi Great River Road is an all-year route but in the fall some of the views are at their very best – as in this section at Brainerd, Minnesota.

MUST SEE

On such a long journey there are unlimited points of interest but the source of the **Mississippi** – **Lake Itasca** – should certainly be visited.

The **museums** at **Grand Rapids** and then at **Minneapolis** and **St. Paul** should not be missed.

Wildlife is abundant along the river but the **Driftless Region** of Wisconsin and Illinois and, further south, the **floodplains** at Toolesboro should not be missed.

Mark Twain's name is inextricably linked to the Mississippi so a stop at his home town of **Hannibal** is essential. And when you reach St. Louis, you won't be able to miss the massive **Gateway Arch** but this city, first founded by the French, has a wonderful **cathedral**, **churches** and **abbeys**, a unique city **cuisine**, and many fine **jazz**, **ragtime**, and **blues** music venues.

Below: Overlook from Buena Vista City Park above Alma, Wisconsin, and the Mississippi river along Highway 35 or the Great River Road.

Once across the state line into Wisconsin you might choose to stop and visit the Fort Crawford Museum in Prairie du Chien, Grandad Bluff at La Crosse (La Crosse also boasts the world's biggest six-pack of beer), and Buena Vista Park in Alma. The northern part of Wisconsin is fertile and an important part of the USA's breadbasket but further south the landscape changes radically in what is called the Driftless Region. The area stretches into Illinois and is an area of fabulous views from the heights, steep and deep canyons, and teeming wildlife – here is part of the Mississippi Flyway where huge flocks of birds fly over the river on their migrations north in spring and south in fall.

The GRR then passes through Iowa, Illinois, and Missouri. In Iowa, at Toolesboro, three rivers come together where the Iowa and Cedar join the Mississippi. It's an area of huge floodplains and marshes where wildlife is all around. This was also an area favored by Native Americans because of its abundant fish, waterfowl, and game.

Into Illinois, you might want to stop at the old town of Nauvoo, which was once home to 6,000 Mormon believers before they moved

on to Utah. Then after crossing into Missouri an essential stop is Mark Twain's hometown of Hannibal which offers museums, riverboat rides, and statues of his famous Tom Sawyer and Huckleberry Finn characters.

Further south, the Illinois River joins the Mississippi, then look out for the massive scenic limestone bluffs between Grafton and Alton and the delightfully historic old village of Elsah before the GRR makes its way toward St. Louis. The Missouri River also joins the Mississippi here, after which the nature of the river changes as from here southward there are no further locks and dams – the last of the 29 locks on the upper reaches of the river is at Granite City, Illinois. Once in St. Louis, you can't miss the massive Gateway Arch which dominates the skyline but there is so much more to this city – vibrant culture, top level sports, live jazz and blues clubs, the famous Bellefontaine Cemetery, the Sophia Sachs Butterfly House, and even the Anheuser-Busch Brewery.

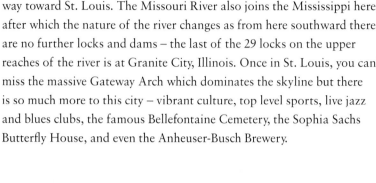

Right: The historic Mormon Temple in Nauvoo, Illinois.

MISSISSIPPI GREAT RIVER ROAD II
TENNESSEE – LOUISIANA

Once south of St. Louis the GRR crosses the Mississippi into Chester, then passes through the Shawnee National Forest out of sight of the river but the raised roadways and occasional levees mean you will know you are not far from what is by now a mile wide expanse of water. Then, just north of Cairo, there is the Horseshoe Lake Conservation Area which provides a fine example of how, as river erosion creates a new channel, an oxbow lake is created. It provides a home for literally millions of wildfowl.

ONCE THE OHIO RIVER JOINS THE MISSISSIPPI, THE GRR MOVES INTO KENTUCKY FOR A SHORT WHILE – AROUND 60 MILES (97 KM) OF SCENIC AND MAINLY RURAL COUNTRYSIDE – AND THEN INTO TENNESSEE. After crossing the state line, again the GRR runs in a scenic, rural stretch until around half way to Memphis when the outlook changes to a mix of old cotton fields and pine woodland interspersed with mobile home parking lots, gaudy commercial strips, and chain hotels and motels.

Memphis itself is an important US city – the one that first provided the world with the drive-in restaurant, the supermarket, and, of course, Elvis Presley. It was also the home of the original Sun Records and Stax Records studios. This is the place to take in some music and

MUST SEE

Memphis, where you will find **Elvis Presley's Graceland**, the original **Stax** and **Sun City** recording studios and the **National Civil Rights Museum** built where **Dr Martin Luther King** was assassinated, cannot be missed.

There's plenty more **blues**, **jazz**, and **country music** to be found in Mississippi, particularly between **Greenville** and **Greenwood**.

Further south check out **Vicksburg** and **Port Gibson** and give yourself plenty of time to savour the delights of **New Orleans**.

visit Elvis's home at Graceland but also don't miss the National Civil Rights Museum in Mulberry Street where Dr. Martin Luther King was assassinated in 1968.

The GRR now flows on south into Mississippi and through the cotton fields of the Mississippi Delta. The cotton is especially visible at harvest time in the fall when vast bales are created at the edges of the fields ready for transportation. This is also, of course, the home of blues, jazz, country, and rock 'n' roll music. The area between Greenville and Greenwood is especially important in the history of the blues where you can find museums and graves of the likes of Robert Johnson, BB King, and Muddy Waters.

After Vicksburg – scene of one of the longest sieges of the Civil War as the city's Confederates stood up to Union attempts to gain control of

the Mississippi River – the GRR follows US-61, the path of the "Great Migration" followed by some five million black sharecroppers to the industrialized north after World War I.

Thirty miles (49 km) south of Vicksburg is Port Gibson, a town spared from destruction during the Civil War because General Grant decreed it was "too beautiful to burn". Worth a visit is the First Presbyterian Church (known as the "Church of the Golden Hand" thanks to the gold-leafed hand on its steeple pointing to heaven), not least because its interior is lit by chandeliers from the steamboat

Above: The National Civil Rights Museum, where Dr. Martin Luther King was killed.

Left: Seemingly endless cotton fields in the Mississippi Delta.

Far left: The *Natchez* steamboat on the Mississippi River at New Orleans.

Above: New Orleans' famous Bourbon Street in the French Quarter.

Far right: A satellite image shows the Mississippi as it flows through New Orleans (shown as the white area, upper left) then down through the Delta and out into the Gulf of Mexico.

From: Memphis

To: New Orleans

Roads: All signposted as one of America's National Scenic Byways

Distance: 868 miles (1,396 km)

Driving Time: 18 hours

When To Go: Year-round

Robert E Lee, winner of the famous 1970 steamboat race from New Orleans to St. Louis.

Finally, into Louisiana, where it becomes more difficult to work out where the land starts and the waters end. The GRR crosses the Mississippi four times between St. Francisville and New Orleans and passes Baton Rouge, where a massively colorful hot air balloon festival is held every August, before moving into Cajun Country.

It's an area well worth exploring for the wildlife in its bayous, its unique spicy cuisine, and its massive sugarcane plantations. Good places to visit are St. Martinville, New Iberia – home of the famous Tabasco sauce – and Breaux Bridge which dubs itself the "Crayfish Capital of the World".

Louisiana is the state of giant levees and massive expanses of standing water and, indeed, by the time you reach New Orleans the road is as much as six feet (1.8 m) below sea level. The city is still recovering from Hurricane Katrina but the multi-cultural heritage of New Orleans is never far below the surface and the French Quarter, the heart of the old city, should not be missed – and if you can arrange to visit during Mardi Gras, so much the better.

From New Orleans it's another 75 miles (120 km) to Venice and the Delta National Wildlife Refuge way down south at the very mouth of the Mississippi on the Gulf of Mexico.

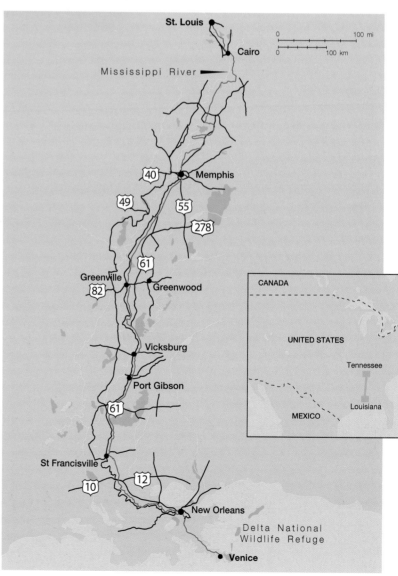

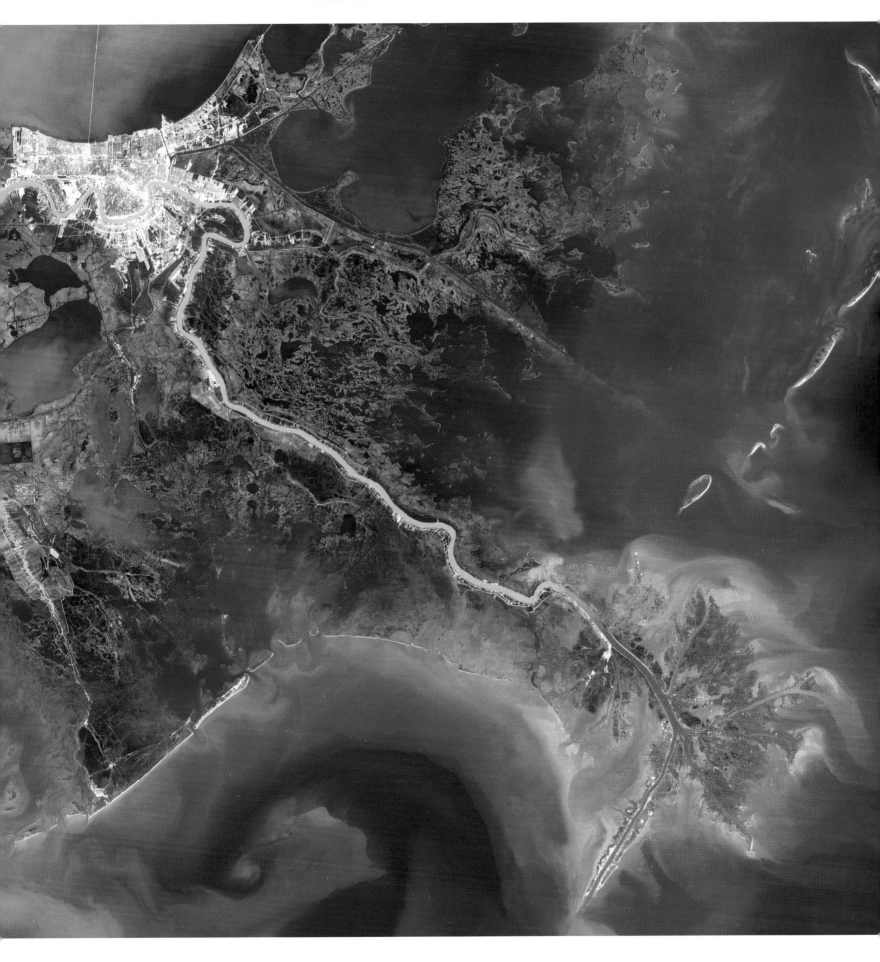

ROUTE 66
ILLINOIS – CALIFORNIA

Route 66 is the most famous road in the USA, yet much of it no longer exists. It was first established on November 11, 1926, and ran from Chicago in Illinois through Missouri, Kansas, Oklahoma, Texas, New Mexico, Arizona, and California, finishing up in Los Angeles on the Pacific Coast 2,448 miles (3,940 km) later.

EVEN IN THOSE EARLY DAYS, ROUTE 66 WAS CONSTANTLY CHANGED AND IMPROVED AS NEW BRIDGES AND BY-PASSES WERE BUILT TO MAKE THE ROAD SHORTER AND SAFER. One change actually lengthened Route 66 when the finishing point moved from downtown Los Angeles to Santa Monica.

Route 66 soon became known as the "Main Street of America" as business people moved west to seek new opportunities. In the 1930s it became an important path for migrants escaping the Dust Bowl of the Midwest and searching for new opportunities in the promised land of California.

The road swiftly became an icon of American culture, taking center stage in pop songs such as Nat King Cole's (and later the Rolling Stones') "Route 66"; in literature such as John Steinbeck's *Grapes of Wrath* where Route 66 was described as "the mother road, the road of flight"; and the popular TV show *Route 66* in the 1960s. But as the Interstate Highway System was developed in the USA, Route 66 became less and less relevant

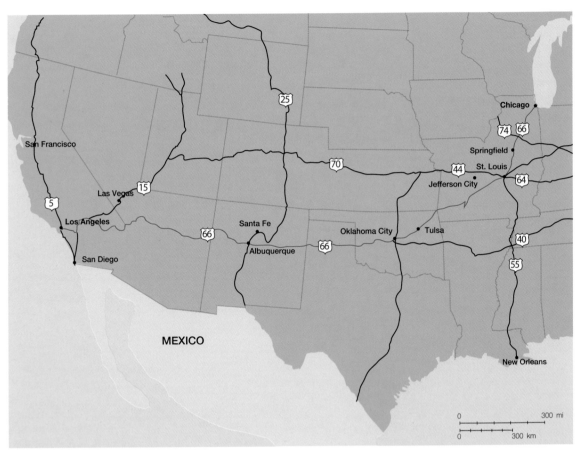

From: Chicago

To: Los Angeles

Roads: Route 66

Distance: 2,448 miles (3,940 km)

Driving Time: 7 days

When To Go: Year-round; but bad weather could affect the early part in mid-winter

Far left: Sections of the original Route 66 can still be found, as here close to the Arizona / California border.

Below: The Route 66 Museum in Clinton, Oklahoma, which depicts the rise and fall of the Main Street of America.

and US 66 was officially removed from the US Highway System on June 27, 1985. And yet Route 66 refused to die. Sections of the old road that passed through Illinois, Missouri, New Mexico, and Arizona were later designated National Scenic Byways and given the new name of "Historic Route 66". In the same way sections in California have been designated either "State Route 66" or "Historic Route 66" and all along the length of the old route, sections are preserved for posterity.

In 1999, President Clinton signed the National Route 66 Preservation Bill which provided up to $10 million in matching fund grants for preserving and restoring what remains of the famous road and its historic features – including motels, neon signs, service stations, and what were at the time America's first fast food restaurants. What will not be found are many "Route 66" signs – simply because of trophy and souvenir hunters. And so now many of the signs are stencilled onto the road itself.

With a bit of research and a good map, much of the old route can still be traced though it will take a week or more to cover the whole of the journey and allow time to visit many of the fascinating historic sights along the way.

From Chicago to St. Louis the road cuts through miles of cornfields, then at Springfield and in the smaller towns beyond some sections of Route 66 have been well preserved.

One of the best preserved sections runs between Springfield, Missouri, and Tulsa in Oklahoma. Oklahoma also boasts some sections which are still in their original format, of a 9 foot (2.75 m) wide single paved lane with gravel shoulders to each side to allow for passing traffic.

There are also good original sections at Flagstaff, Arizona, and then from Seligman to Kingman in the same state. Then, in California, much of the old Route 66 has survived intact and is marked along its 315 mile (507 km) length by Historic Route 66 signage, across the Mojave Desert to San Bernardino and on through Pasadena to Los Angeles via Beverly Hills (where Will Rogers was once mayor), and where the Santa Monica Boulevard becomes Sunset Boulevard to downtown LA and finally to Santa Monica on the coast.

MUST SEE

The Steak & Shake Drive-in, a classic Route 66 burger joint between Bloomington and Normal.

Stop by the **Original Brick Road** at Auburn and the **Mustang Corrall** between Springfield and St. Louis.

There's the **Mississippi River** and **Old Chain of Rocks Bridge** at Edwardsville, the **Will Rogers Museum** at Claremore, and the **Route 66 Museum** in Clinton, Oklahoma.

Also find time to see the **Cadillac Ranch** at Amarillo, Santa Fe, in New Mexico, **Wigwam Motels** at Holbrook, Arizona, and **San Bernardino** in California.

Above left: One of the places where the original brick road can still be seen is in downtown Winslow, Arizona.

Right: Route 66-era classic American cars parked outside the Wigwam Motel in Holbrook, Arizona.

Following pages: Cadillac Ranch in Amarillo, Texas, is a bizarre sculpture consisting of half buried 1950s Cadillac cars.

MIAMI TO KEY WEST
FLORIDA

From Miami, take the Florida Turnpike south signposted to the Florida Keys, then follow US 1 South for around 22 miles (35 km) until you reach Key Largo, the first of the long archipelago of islands that make up the Florida Keys. By now the road has changed its name to the Overseas Highway which is designated by small green marker signs that start just outside Florida City at number 127 and finish in Key West at 0. More importantly, the Overseas Highway was designated by the US Congress in 1991 as one of only 30 All-American Roads in the USA – the country's most stunning and scenic routes.

THE OVERSEAS HIGHWAY, WHICH OPENED IN 1938 FOLLOWING THE ROUTE OF THE RAILROAD ORIGINALLY CONSTRUCTED BY OIL MILLIONAIRE HENRY FLAGLER IN 1912, IS UNIQUE IN THAT MUCH OF IT IS OVER WATER. It involves 42 bridges linking the various keys between Key Largo and Key West, the longest of which spans 6.79 miles (10.9 km) of open water at Marathon – the famous Seven Mile Bridge. Small wonder that the route was described as "the eighth wonder of the world".

Driving the route for the first time, despite the abundance of natural beauty of the beaches, palms, mudflats, distant islands, pelicans in the sky, and multi-colored tropical fish in the waters, it's the sheer brilliance of the engineering that takes center stage as the unbelievably long bridges stretch across the calm waters with the Atlantic Ocean to the left and the Gulf of Mexico to the right.

Key Largo bills itself as the scuba diving capital of the world thanks to the John Pennekamp Coral Reef Park, the Florida Keys National Marine Sanctuary, and the wreck of the former US Navy ship *Speigal Grove*. There's plenty of underwater action for snorkelers too and glass-bottomed boat trips for those who don't want to get their feet wet.

Moving south to Islamorada Key, there might be time to stop off at the famous Snappers Waterfront Restaurant, often frequented by celebrities. For a more traditional experience the Kona Kai hotel is an original 1940s holiday resort, though considerably upgraded to suit 21st century tastes.

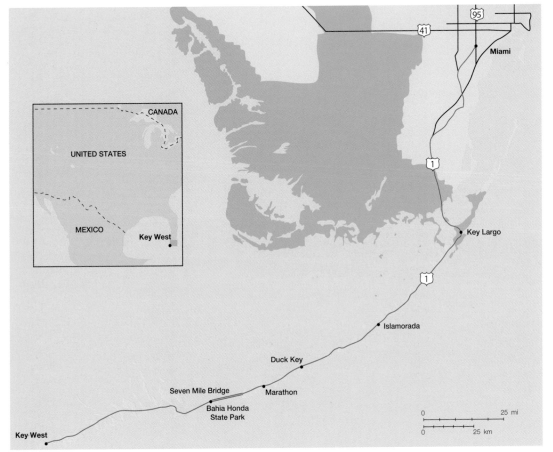

Above: The Bahia Honda State Park in the lower Florida Keys covers most of the island. It's a place of fine beaches, unpolluted waters, and abundant wildlife. It's also a great place for snorkeling off the beach for views of brightly colored reef fish and larger Barracuda, rays, and nurse sharks.

Far left: The iconic Seven Mile Bridge is one of the wonders of the Overseas Highway. The first bridge was finished in 1912 but was damaged by a hurricane in 1935 and later completely re-built.

From: Miami

To: Key West

Roads: US Route 1, Overseas Highway

Distance: 159 miles (256 km)

Driving Time: Time: 3–4 hours

When To Go: Year-round but be aware of late summer and fall hurricane season

Continue past Duck Key – which offers the Lost and Found Reef for divers – where you can make the short detour to Hawks Cay to swim with dolphins. It might be worth another quick detour in Marathon to sample one of the famous lobster Reuben sandwiches served at the Keys Fisheries and Marina. Also from Marathon there is a ferry to the historic Pigeon Key which is where the workers constructing Henry Flagler's railroad lived. The island is positioned under the midpoint of the Old Seven Mile Bridge which, when it was built between 1909 and 1912, was one of the world's longest bridge spans. It was badly damaged in a hurricane in 1935 after which the railroad was closed and work started on the Overseas Highway.

MUST SEE

At Key Largo call in at the **John Pennekamp Coral Reef Park** and the **Florida Keys National Marine Sanctuary**.

At Marathon there is the magnificent **Seven Mile Bridge** and you can also catch a ferry to historic **Pigeon Key**.

Further south you'll find **Bahia Honda State Park**.

And once in Key West there's the **Historic District**, Ernest Hemingway's house, **Casa Marine Resort**, and the **Mel Fisher Maritime Museum**.

Right: The Ernest Hemingway home and Museum is housed in the quiet and shaded property that was the famous writer's residence from 1931 to 1939.

Below left: Along with its famous laid-back culture, Key West – at the very end of the long line of Florida Keys – is renowned for its magnificent sunsets.

Below: One of the many easily-accessible dive sites is the *Doc DeMille* wreck off Key Largo.

Following pages: Colorful conch houses in Key West, Florida.

Further south, the Bahia Honda State Park offers fine beaches, clear waters, and stunning displays of wildlife, all with the backdrop of one of Flagler's surviving railway bridges.

The end of the road is Key West, famous for its laid-back lifestyle, clapperboard houses, unusual shops, Key West Lime Pies, Sloppy Joe's bar, writer Ernest Hemingway's house and the Hemingway Museum, and wonderful sunsets. The Key West Historic District includes Mallory Square and Duval Street which are the main tourist destinations. For those interested in history, the Casa Marine Resort, which used to house military personnel during World War II, is now a museum that recalls the days when the only way to reach Key West was by boat or Flagler's train. The Mel Fisher Maritime Museum specialises in treasures raised from the seabed. For good measure, Key West is also a dive and sailing enthusiast's dream.

BLUE RIDGE PARKWAY
VIRGINIA – NORTH CAROLINA

Construction of the Blue Ridge Parkway started in 1935 but was not completed until 1987. Its meandering 469 mile (755 km) route is banned to all commercial traffic – and to all commercial billboards – and the route has become firmly established as one of the greatest US scenic drives, attracting more visitors to the area than the Grand Canyon each year. They come for the sheer beauty of the Appalachian Highlands and the stunning contrasts between rocky mountains, verdant meadows, forests, lakes, and pastures.

OFTEN NAMED "AMERICA'S FAVOURITE DRIVE," IT IS A ROAD TRIP THAT SHOULD BE TAKEN AT A GENTLE PACE, ALLOWING MAXIMUM ENJOYMENT OF THE EVER-CHANGING SCENERY. It is well worth checking the Blue Ridge Parkway website (www.blueridgeparkway.org) in advance to plan your journey and potential stops because there is so much to see and do along this route. In general though, take the journey in spring for wildflowers and azaleas; in summer for the stunning rhododendrons at higher elevations; or in the fall for the magnificent reds and yellows as the deciduous trees change color. There's plenty to see in wintertime, too,

though higher passes may be closed by snow. Again, the website will give up-to-date information.

The route starts at Rockfish Gap and the first of many visitor centers can be found at Milepost 5.8, at Humpback Rocks. Astonishing views

Right: The unspoilt Blue Ridge Parkway National Park near Asheville, North Carolina.

Below: Linn Cove Viaduct, which snakes around the Grandfather Mountains, was the last part of the road to be constructed, in 1987.

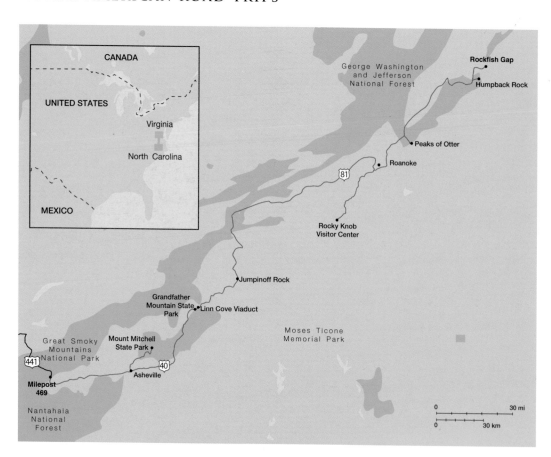

From: Rockfish Gap

To: Smoky Mountains National Park

Roads: Blue Ridge Parkway

Distance: 469 miles (755 km)

Driving Time: 3 days

When To Go: Year Round but check for winter road closures

Below left: Mabry Mill, at Milepost 176 is one of the Blue Ridge Parkway's iconic buildings. It first opened in 1908 as a gristmill for grinding corn, then a lumber mill was built and finally a blacksmith's shop.

Right: The Mile High Swinging Bridge in the Grandfather Mountains, the highest suspension bridge in the USA.

MUST SEE

Along this route across the **Appalachian Mountains** from **Shenandoah National Park** in Virginia to the **Great Smoky Mountains National Park** of North Carolina, expect to see massive panoramic views interspersed with lush green meadows and thick, dark forests. Don't miss the mountain scenery at **Otter Visitor Center**, the views at **Jumpinoff Rocks** and **Linn Cove Viaduct**, or from the **Mile-High Swinging Bridge** and **Mount Mitchell State Park** with its observation tower – the highest point east of the **Mississippi River**.

can also be found from Apple Orchard Mountain Overlook at Milepost 76.5, and again at Mileposts 84 through to 87, which offer panoramas of the three Peaks of Otter – Sharp Top, Flat Top, and Harkening Hill – rising above Abbott Lake.

After passing Roanoke, the next hundred miles or so provide pretty, pastoral scenes of small farms, pioneer cabins, and rural landscapes. As you head south, however, the vistas start becoming more dramatic once again. At Rocky Knob (Mileposts 167 to 174) there's a campground and visitor center. At Milepost 167.1 more adventurous travelers may wish to park and hike the steep and difficult trail than leads down into Rocky Castle Gorge and up over the 3,572 foot (1,089 m) Rocky Knob.

At Milepost 216.7 you will cross from Virginia into North Carolina and in many ways this next section is the most dramatic and rewarding part of the trip. Here, the Blue Ridge Parkway snakes over the Blue Ridge Mountains, then higher over the Black Mountains, and finally into the Great Smoky Mountains National Park.

At Milepost 260.6 a short trail leads to the summit of Jumpinoff Rocks where more magnificent views stretch for miles. Soon after, at Mileposts 292 to 295, the Moses H. Cone Memorial Park offers numerous mountain hiking trails. The Southern Highlands Craft Center at Milepost 294 showcases traditional Appalachian crafts during the summer months.

Further along, at Milepost 304, the road crosses Linn Cove Viaduct, the last part of the route to be built in 1987 and a stunning feat of civil engineering that takes the Parkway around Grandfather Mountain.

Here, the driver receives the impression of driving through treetops. It is undoubtedly one of the highlights of the journey. Grandfather Mountain, at 5,946 feet (1,812 m), hosts a private park with numerous trails as well as the iconic Mile-High Swinging Bridge. This is the USA's highest suspension bridge, built in 1952. Its 228 foot (69 m) span crosses an 80 foot (24 m) gorge to provide visitors with superb views from Linville Peak on Grandfather Mountain. A little further along the Parkway, the Linville Falls can be seen at Milepost 316.3.

Milepost 355.4 leads to Mount Mitchell State Park where there is a mountaintop viewing tower. Helpfully, drivers can approach close to the top of the 6,684 foot (2,037 m) summit of Mount Mitchell, the highest point in the USA east of the Mississippi River. The highest point on the Parkway itself is at Milepost 431, where the road climbs to 6,047 feet (1,843 m) above sea level.

This is a journey that any driver will want to go on and on, but all good things come to an end and the Blue Ridge Parkway's arrives at Milepost 469 where it joins US-441 at the entrance to the Smoky Mountains National Park.

Following pages: Craggy Pinnacle Tunnel is one of 26 constructed along the Blue Ridge Parkway

DARE TRAIL
NORTH CAROLINA

North Carolina's Outer Banks is a chain of barrier islands extending almost 200 miles (320 km) down the coast and comprising four main islands: Bodie, Roanoke, Hatteras, and Ocracoke. Some 1,500 wrecks have been recorded in these notoriously dangerous waters, giving rise to the region's nickname: "Graveyard of the Atlantic". All the islands are accessible by car though visitors will need to take a ferry to reach Ocracoke at the end of the trail. The speed limit on Highway 12 is 35 mph and even lower (20-25 mph) on Ocracoke, so this is not a drive to rush. Drivers should relax and soak up the atmosphere of this very special area.

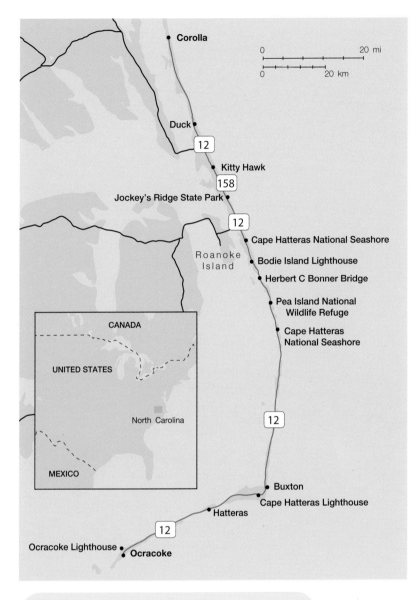

From: Corolla

To: Ocracoke

Roads: Highway 12, Route 158

Distance: 114 miles (183 km)

Driving Time: 3-4 hours

When To Go: Year round, though can be stormy in wintertime and very busy in summertime. Best in spring and fall.

Right: Wild colonial Spanish mustangs on the shores of the Outer Banks in Corolla. They have lived here some 500 years, perhaps left behind by Spanish explorers.

Left: The elegant Herbert Bonner Bridge connects Bodie Island to Pea Island. The 2.7 mile (4.3 km) construction was completed in 1963.

START IN COROLLA AND MAKE THE EFFORT TO CLIMB THE 214 STAIRS TO THE TOP OF THE CURRITUCK BEACH LIGHTHOUSE from where the lucky might see some of Corolla's famous wild horses, descended from Spanish mustangs brought here hundreds of years ago.

The first stretch of Highway 12, from Corolla to Duck, takes travelers past some amazing upmarket beach houses. After passing Duck, take Route 158, which runs alongside Highway 12 ("The Beach Road"). At Milepost 7.5, you will arrive at the Wright Brothers National Memorial. It was from this spot that, in 1903, Orville and Wilbur Wright made the first ever powered flight in the Kill Devil Hills, a few miles south of Kitty Hawk. Their Wright Flyer 1 flew 120 feet (37 m), reaching 10 feet (3 m) above the ground. A fascinating stop, the memorial has numerous exhibits and movies, as well as full-sized replicas of the 1903 plane and an earlier 1902 glider.

Rejoin Highway 12 and continue south to Jockey's Ridge State Park, a large recreational area on the dunes that contains the highest sand dunes on the whole of the USA's Atlantic coast. A little further south, travelers might wish to take another detour to Roanoke Island. This is where the very first English settlers lived during the reign of Queen Elizabeth I. In fact, the name "Dare Trail" derives from Virginia Dare, whose birth in August 1587 made her the first English child to

be born in the New World. She has since become an important figure in American folklore, mainly because nothing is known of her fate, nor that of her fellow colonists, all of whom disappeared from Roanoke sometime between her birthdate and 1590, when the colony was found to be deserted. The story of this lost colony is well told at the Fort Raleigh National Historic Site.

From here to the very end of the trail, the route passes through the Cape Hatteras National Seashore, an unspoilt and largely undeveloped area of beaches, creeks, and inlets. Some six miles after entering the park you will see the Bodie Island Lighthouse, built in 1872 to replace an earlier lighthouse that was destroyed by Confederate troops in 1861. The Pea Island National Wildlife Reserve offers another excellent place to break the journey. Here, travelers will see countless sea birds, including geese, ducks, ospreys, and swans.

About 20 miles (32 km) further south travelers will see the distinctive stripes of the Cape Hatteras Lighthouse, the tallest brick lighthouse in the USA and a famous landmark since it was built in 1870. Because of erosion of the beach it was moved inland in 1999, but it remains a spectacular structure. Next up is the bustling town of Buxton on Hatteras Island, full of restaurants, boutique hotels, bike and watercraft hire shops, and tackle shops. Continue on Highway 12 to Hatteras Village at the end of the island. From here, take the 40-minute ferry ride across to Ocracoke Island and the end of the line.

MUST SEE

Travelers should take time to see the four famous lighthouses that protect shipping in this area where the ocean meets the land. **The Currituck Beach Lighthouse** in Corolla, **Cape Hatteras Light**, and **Bodie Island Lighthouse** are open to visitors, while the **Ocracoke Lighthouse** can be photographed from outside.

The Wright Brothers National Memorial, on the site of their first flight, is also a must-see. Otherwise, travelers can enjoy the sights provided by miles of unspoiled beaches, seabirds, and other wildlife along these barrier island coasts.

Ocracoke's 16-mile stretch of coastline boasts different environments: sand dunes to the east overlook the ocean while salt water marshland to the west overlooks Pamlico Sound. Though the ferry from Hatteras Island is free, not many drivers venture this far and there is a quieter, more relaxed atmosphere here. In fact, most people arriving on Ocracoke prefer to continue their journey on foot or bicycle. If you choose to venture this far, make sure to visit the Ocracoke Lighthouse. It is the oldest operational lighthouse in the USA – first built in 1823 – and also the shortest at a mere 75 feet (23 m) in height. Unfortunately, it is not open to visitors but information about the lighthouse and the region's heritage can be found at the Ocracoke Preservation Society Museum.

Left: Ocracoke Island, which can only be reached via a 40 minute ferry ride, is at the very end of the Dare Trail.

Right: Bodie Island Lighthouse was built in 1872, replacing an earlier structure that was destroyed by Confederate troops.

CAPE COD ROUTE 6A
MASSACHUSETTS

Massachusetts Route 6A, which runs the length of Cape Cod along its northern coastline, is often called the Old King's Highway. In fact, the route is an extension of the King's Highway that Charles II of England ordered to be built between Charleston, South Carolina, and Boston, Massachusetts. It follows a path that was first a Native American trail, then a cart track used by early settlers. Today, it offers a glimpse of America's past. As well as the beaches and wildlife that can be seen along the route there are numerous charming historic towns and villages replete with stately homes, old houses, lovely gardens, and atmospheric graveyards.

FROM SAGAMORE IN THE EAST, CROSS THE SAGAMORE BRIDGE ONTO CAPE COD AND FOLLOW THE 6A INTO SANDWICH, THE OLDEST TOWN ON CAPE COD AND ONE THAT WAS ESTABLISHED BY PURITAN SETTLERS IN 1637. Dating to those times are Hoxie House, believed to be the Cape's oldest saltbox house, and the Dexter Grist Mill, both of which were built in the mid-1600s. This was once also the location of the biggest glass factory in the USA. Its history can be traced in the Sandwich Glass Museum.

Keep going toward Barnstable, a town established in 1639 and an early fishing port that took full advantage of the riches of the Grand Banks fishing area. Encompassing several villages within its boundaries, many of Barnstable's finest houses were once home to wealthy sea captains. There are yet more fine historic houses to be seen in the next town of Yarmouth and nearby Yarmouth Port.

Above: The extensive saltmarshes on Cape Cod are an important haven for wildfowl .

Far left: Dexter's Grist Mill was first built in 1637 and remained a working grist mill until 1881. The current building was restored in 1961 and is now open to the public.

Such wealthy seafarers also made their homes in Dennis and Brewster, where you will find the Cape Cod Museum of Natural History. A short detour from Dennis onto Old Bass River Road and then into Scargo Hill Road is worthwhile. It takes you to the top of Scargo Hill, the highest point on Cape Cod from where you can see for miles. Past Brewster is Nickerson State Park, the largest inland nature reserve on Cape Cod, covering some 1,900 acres (7.7 km²).

Above: The town of Truro was named by English settlers after Truro in Cornwall. The English pilgrims first visited the area in 1620.

Right: The Marconi site, from where the first trans-Atlantic radio message was sent by Guglielmo Marconi in 1903. This is also the place where the *Titanic*'s SOS calls were received in 1912.

Far right: The first Race Point Lighthouse was built at the very far tip of Cape Cod in 1816 and replaced by the current 45 feet (13.7 m) structure in 1876.

Following pages: Provincetown Wharf at sunset. Provincetown is where the Pilgrims first landed and today is a bustling harbor town that's a vibrant fishing and whale-watching center.

Once past the town of Orleans – which is where some of the cape's most popular beaches can be found – Route 6A shares Route 6 as it travels through the Cape Cod National Seashore, a 68 square mile (176km²) expanse of salt marshes, tidal inlets, and pine woods. It's worth making a stop at the Salt Pond Visitor Center in Eastham to see the salt marshes and tidal inlets, which are teeming with wildfowl.

A little further on, at South Wellfleet, there is another fascinating top to be made at the Marconi Station Site, where Guglielmo Marconi

sent the first radio message across the Atlantic Ocean to Cornwall in the far west of the United Kingdom in 1903. Interestingly, a radio station was active here until 1917 and it was here that SOS calls from the *RMS Titanic* were received in 1912, allowing the station to alert *RMS Carpathia* to the unfolding tragedy.

Continue along Route 6 through Truro and North Truro into countryside where Cape Cod becomes less developed and reveals yet more of its natural splendors. After North Truro the road splits and

From: East Sandwich

To: Provincetown

Roads: MA-6A/6

Distance: 62 miles (100 km)

Driving Time: 1-2 hours

When To Go: Year round. Best in spring and fall, can be busy in summer

MUST SEE

All along this route are magnificent views of the ocean, sand dunes, and salt marshes. Other highlights include **Sandwich** and **Barnstable** harbors, the **Cape Cod National Seashore**, the **Marconi Station Site**, and **Head of the Meadow Beach**.

In Provincetown, the **Pilgrim Monument** and **Provincetown Museum** are well worth a visit, as is the furthest tip of Cape Cod, where **Race Point Beach** and **Race Point Light** can be found.

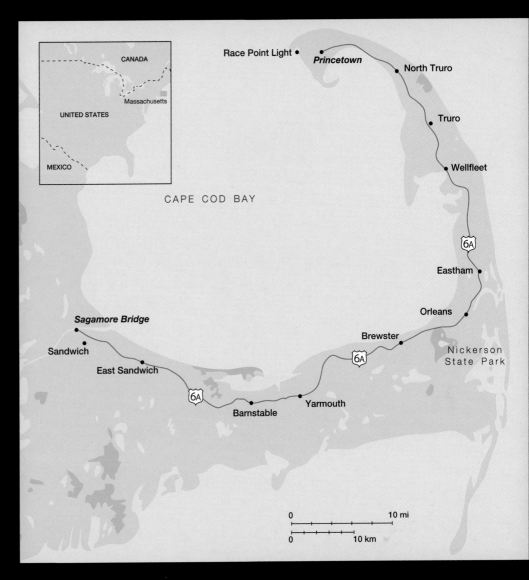

drivers return to Route 6A once more. One of the most beautiful beaches on the cape is Head of the Meadow Beach, which can be found just beyond North Truro.

Further along the road is Provincetown, at the far north of Cape Cod. Another fishing village, this is where the *Mayflower* pilgrims first landed in 1620 before continuing on to their final destination of Plymouth. The town now boasts a museum that covers the event as well as a massive 252 foot (77 meter) granite tower that commemorates the arrival. From the top of the tower, which was completed in 1910, there are wonderful views in all directions over the Cape Cod landscape. Provincetown was also once an important whaling station and, today, visitors can hop onboard whale-watching boats offering the opportunity to see these magnificent creatures at close quarters during the season, which roughly lasts from April to September.

Also worth a visit at the end of the road is Race Point Beach and Light, right on the very tip of the Cape. The lighthouse was built in 1816 and was one of the first to be fitted with a rotating beacon.

MOHAWK TRAIL
MASSACHUSETTS

The Mohawk Trail in Massachusetts, between the Connecticut and Hudson valleys, became one of the very earliest scenic auto routes in the United States when it opened in 1914 as a narrow gravel road. It followed the path of a trading route used for thousands of years by Native Americans and today there's plenty of history along the way.

THE ROAD HAS BEEN WIDENED AND UPGRADED SINCE 1914 BUT IT STILL WINDS AND MEANDERS GENTLY THROUGH THE MASSACHUSETTS HINTERLAND, through dark forests, green pastures, and historic old towns as it crosses and follows no fewer than five waterways – the Millers, Connecticut, Green, Deerfield, and Hoosic rivers.

Williamstown, at the western end of the route, is home to the Chapin Library of Rare Books on the campus of Williams College.

Anyone interested in American history will want to take a look: the library holds original printings of the four founding documents of the United States of America.

After leaving Williamstown, look for a right turn to Mount Greylock State Reservation. Mount Greylock itself, at 3,491 feet (1064 m), is the highest point in Massachusetts. The road offers many viewing points where you can stop and admire the landscapes of Berkshire County. At the very top, travelers won't be able to miss the massive granite Veterans

Memorial Tower (roads are closed out of season). Anyone climbing to the observation deck at the top will be rewarded with views stretching as far as the Catskills in New York, the Adirondacks, Vermont's Green Mountains, and New Hampshire's Mount Monadnock.

From here, take MA-2 to North Adams, a vibrant center for the arts. A detour from here into the Natural Bridge State Park is recommended. The park contains a famous natural marble bridge, its gap cut over millions of years as part of the 60-foot- (18-m-) deep gorge created by the fast-flowing waters of Hudson Brook.

The Mohawk Trail truly starts after North Adams. Drivers should prepare themselves for the Hairpin Turn, where the trail heads steeply uphill to what the Native Americans called Spirit Mountain. Today, it

Right: The Massachusetts Veterans War Memorial Tower at the top of Mount Greylock, the highest point in the State at 3,489 ft (751 m).

Left: The Connecticut River, Canal, and Reservoir, at Turners Falls.

From: Williamstown

To: Greenfield

Roads: Mohawk Trail (MA 2)

Distance: 69 miles (111 km)

Driving Time: 2-3 hours

When To Go: Year round

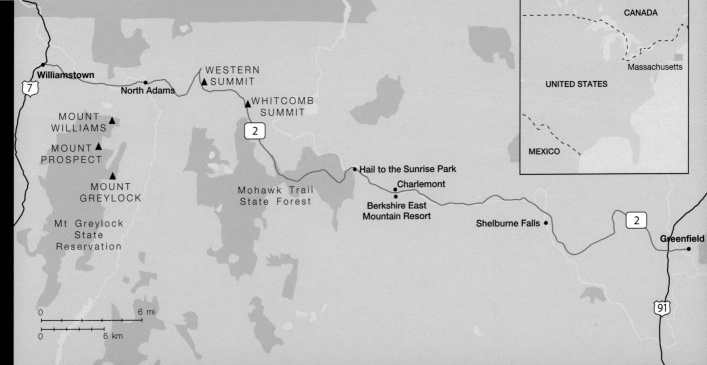

boasts the more prosaic name of the Western Summit. Stop here for far-reaching views of Massachusetts and southern Vermont, including mounts Prospect, Greylock, and Williams in the distance.

The road continues climbing all the way to Whitcomb Summit, the highest point of the trail at 2,173 feet (662 m), from where both the Green Mountains of Vermont and Monadnock Mountain in New Hampshire can be seen on a clear day. Further along MA-2 you will come to the Mohawk Trail State Forest, which offers some 6,000 acres (24 km²) of hiking trails, fishing, camping, and other recreational activities. Don't miss the 80 foot (24.3 m) Tannery Falls and the series of cascades that comprise Parker Brooks Falls.

Hail to the Sunrise Park is another interesting place to break the trip. It commemorates the Five Indian Nations and features an impressive bronze statue of a Mohawk Indian raising his arms to the east, welcoming the Great Spirit. Anyone looking for outdoor adventure might also consider a stop at the Berkshire East Mountain Resort. It offers skiing in winter; hiking and mountain biking the rest of the year.

Further down the road is Charlemont where road-trippers will find fishing, boating, and white water rafting on the Deerfield River. A few miles further on, the town of Shelburne Falls is home to the famous Bridge of Flowers. Originally a concrete railway bridge, the structure fell into disrepair after the boom in automobile traffic. Luckily, the cost of demolishing it was deemed too high and in 1929 a women's club banded together to plant the bridge with flowers and shrubs. The transformation was wonderfully successful and, today, the fragrant bridge is open from

Above left: The impressive bronze Mohawk Indian welcoming the Great Spirit in Hail to the Sunrise Park.

Left: The Bridge of Flowers in Shelburne Falls, an abandoned railway bridge transformed in 1929 by a local women's' club.

Above right: From the top of Mount Greylock there are views for miles around but the roads

April to October. From here to the end of the trail in Greenfield travelers will find themselves in maple syrup country. Visit in the early spring and stop at one of the numerous sugar houses where you can see how the sap of the maple trees is tapped and boiled to produce the sweet syrup.

There is yet more scenic beauty to be found at High Ledges Wildlife Sanctuary, which offers hikes amongst abundant wild flowers with panoramic views of the Deerfield Valley and Mount Greylock. A separate trail leads to the top of Massaemett Mountain where it is possible to climb the tower for views over three states – Massachusetts, New Hampshire, and Vermont.

At the end of the Mohawk Trail, Greenfield's historic district is home to museums and atmospheric 19th century buildings. While in Greenfield, travelers should also consider a visit to Poet's Seat Tower, built in 1912 to commemorate local poet Frederick Tuckerman. From here there are superb views over Greenfield itself, as well as the

Connecticut River and Turners Falls. Old Greenfield Village also makes for a fascinating glimpse of old America. Preserved as it would have been in 1895, this archetypal New England museum features a number of shops, offices, and businesses all with original artifacts, signs, and products.

MUST SEE

Another great route for anyone who wishes to take in some stunning scenery and American heritage, highlights of the Mohawk Trail include the **Natural Bridge State Park**, **Western** and **Whitcomb** summits (for their far-reaching views), **Mohawk Trail State Forest**, the **Bridge of Flowers** in Shelburne Falls, the **High Ledges Wildlife Sanctuary**, **Old Greenfield Village**, and **Greenfield's museums**.

CONNECTICUT RIVER BYWAY
VERMONT – MASSACHUSETTS

The Connecticut River Byway takes travelers through 500 miles (805 km) of sumptuous scenery, meandering along the 410 mile (660 km) length of the Connecticut River from its source on the Canadian border, through Vermont, New Hampshire, and Massachusetts. Designated a National Scenic Byway in 2005, it passes through areas of great scenic, cultural, historic, and recreational value.

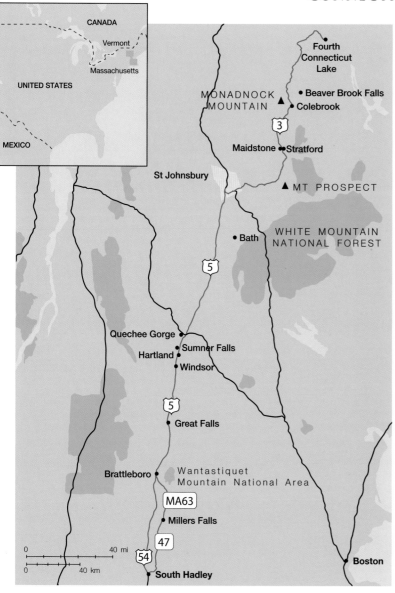

From: West Stewartstown

To: South Hadley

Roads: VT-102, US-5, VT-142, NH-145, US-3, NH-135, NH-10, US-4, NH-123, NH-12, NH-63, MA-63, MA-47

Distance: 498 miles (803 km)

Driving Time: 14 hours to many days

When To Go: Year round but best in summer and fall

Right: The lookout tower on the summit of Mount Prospect in Weeks State Park in New Hampshire.

Left: A short detour to the historic covered bridge at Bath, NH, should not be missed.

IN ITS ENTIRETY, THE ROUTE COMPRISES A NUMBER OF DIFFERENT ROADS, BUT THE WHOLE BYWAY IS WELL SIGNPOSTED WITH DISTINCTIVE BLUE AND WHITE CONNECTICUT RIVER BYWAY SIGNPOSTS. And it's not necessary to drive the whole 500 miles to get a flavor of this experience. Drivers with less time on their hands may wish to choose one or more sections or loops to explore. More detail and individual itineraries are available on the official byway website (www.ctriverbyways.org).

At the most northerly section of the byway, the river is little more than a stream, rising in Fourth Connecticut Lake and passing through a number of lakes – many created by beavers – until it reaches Colebrook in New Hampshire. Covered bridges, waterfalls, and mountains provide the scenic backdrop here for those wishing to stop and take in the sights, and there's a visitor center just north of downtown Colebrook where road-trippers can obtain information about specific attractions (including Beaver Brook Falls and Monadnock Mountain).

Heading south, the Lancaster region offers wonderful views of the Presidential Range of the White Mountains. This is a popular

recreational area, offering winter sports – the USA's first ski school was opened here in the 1940s – hiking, and hunting. Don't miss the 2,059 foot (628 m) Mount Prospect where a lookout tower provides stunning 360 degree views over the Connecticut River Valley, the White and Green mountains, and the Kilkenny range. Again, there is a waypoint center at Lancaster itself for travelers looking for detailed information and excursion ideas.

Yet further south, but still in Vermont, St. Johnsbury boasts New England's most important collection of well-preserved Victorian buildings. Here, you will also find the Fairbanks Museum and Planetarium, which has housed a massive natural history collection since 1889. Nearby Moore and Comerford reservoirs offer boating and fishing in an undeveloped environment overlooked by the White Mountains.

Heading down US-5, it's worth taking a short detour to Bath in New Hampshire to view its historic covered bridge. The oldest covered bridge in the USA, crossing the Ammonoosuc River in Woodsville, is also not to be missed. Woodsville is also where both the Ammonoosuc and Wells rivers join the Connecticut River, offering plenty of fun for white-water enthusiasts.

White River Junction, where the White River joins the Connecticut, has long been an important trading point. More visually impressive is the Quechee Gorge a little further south, where the Ottauquechee River has carved out a gorge reaching depths of 165 feet (50 m). Quechee is also home to the Vermont Institute of Natural Science, an important environmental center. More covered bridges can be found nearby, in Hartland, Plainfield, and Lebanon.

Left: The Quechee Gorge in Windsor County Vermont is at its best as the colors change in the fall months.

Above: The Windsor-Cornish covered bridge that crosses the Connecticut River. Mount Ascutney is in the distance.

Check out Sumner Falls near Hartland, which also attracts white water fans in large numbers. Further south is the town of Windsor, famous for its covered bridge (the country's longest), for being the place where Vermont's first constitution was drawn up, and for the impressive Mount Ascutney which rises to 3,144 feet (958 m). It's the highest monadnock (which means individual mountain, rather than a mountain that is part of a chain) in the east of the USA.

Between Bellows Falls and Walpole, the Connecticut passes through a narrow gorge where, at Great Falls, Native Americans fished for migrating salmon. During the spring, as snow from the surrounding area melts, it often becomes a thunderous torrent. Because the river is so narrow, it's no surprise that the very first bridge over the Connecticut was built here in 1785.

The final section of the byway takes travelers to Brattleboro, originally a military base built in 1724 but now a large town that was popular in the 19th century for its natural mineral waters. From here you can take a detour into the Mount Wantastiquet State Forest, or check out yet more covered bridges in Guilford, Swanzey, and Winchester. The last leg of the route is along the MA-63, through Millers Falls and Montague, then onto MA-47 to journey's end in South Hadley.

ROUTE 100
VERMONT

Route 100 in Vermont runs south-north, from Wilmington not far from the Massachusetts border, to Waitsfield, some 122 miles (196 km) away, then further north to Westfield, close to the Canadian border on the Mad River Valley. It's a route of beautiful mountain scenery, some of the finest fall leaf displays to be found anywhere in the country, and a succession of well-preserved farms, homesteads, villages, and towns. This is archetypal small town America.

IT IS POSSIBLE TO DRIVE FROM WILMINGTON TO WAITSFIELD IN A FEW HOURS, but there are so many places to stop off and see that many drivers take a couple of days over this gentle journey. Route 100 runs alongside the Green Mountain National Forest and is one of the most scenic of all roads in Vermont. Running through pristine wilderness, it rises to the mountains and descends through winding river valleys. For lovers of fall colors, the first two weeks of October are probably the best time to visit but the road is likely to be busy at this time as it's is a very popular "leaf-peeping" route. In summer the road is less crowded and there's no danger of snow and ice, which make driving difficult.

Right: Sugarbush Resort is one of the largest ski areas in New England, and one of many located along the "Skiers Highway".

Below: The Vermont Country Store in Weston opened in 1946 and became one of the USA's first mail order outlets.

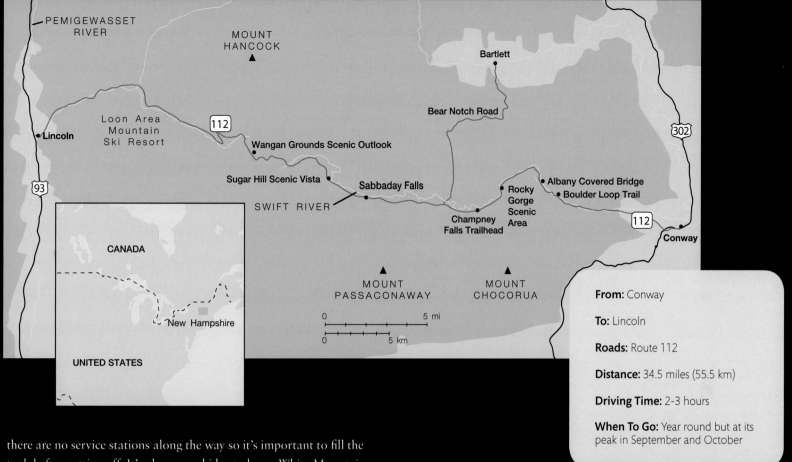

there are no service stations along the way so it's important to fill the tank before setting off. It's also a good idea to buy a White Mountain National Forest Pass as this will be needed for many of the parking areas and trails along the way.

Starting from Conway, head west along Route 112 – following the Swift River through Saco River Valley. After six miles (9.5 km) travelers will arrive at the Albany Covered Bridge, built in 1858. This is one of many picturesque antique structures to be seen along the journey. From here you can take the three-mile (4.85 km) Boulder Loop Trail created during the last Ice Age when glaciers deposited massive granite boulders along its path. There are numerous more hiking trails along the Kancamagus Highway. All offer amazing views of the local scenery and also the possibility of seeing all sorts of wildlife, including deer, moose, foxes, and black bears. This is a region teeming with birdlife, too, including the spectacular green heron.

At the seven-mile (11 km) point, the Swift River Lower Falls is a popular place for a picnic and perhaps even a swim in the river – though the waters remain cool even in high summer. The next parking area is at 9.2 miles (15 km) where the Rocky Gorge Bridge crosses the river. Upstream is an impressive waterfall, while downstream is the scenic Fall Pond. The series of waterfalls called the Champney Falls can be accessed at 10.7 miles (17 km). Travelers parking here will require a pass. The hiking trail to the falls, and another to the Piper Trail, both lead to the top of Mount Chocorua, from where there are splendid panoramic views to be had.

Further along, look for the turn on the right into Bear Notch Road. This road is closed in winter but for the rest of the year makes a pleasing detour up past the Upper Nanamocomuck cross-country skiing trail to the White Mountain Trail and, eventually, the town of Bartlett.

The Russell-Colbath Historic Homestead, at 12.7 miles (20.5 km), is a former farmhouse now converted to a museum that showcases domestic life in this region during the 19th century. A little further on, at 15.6 miles (25 km), are the Sabbaday Falls, easily reached along a short trail from the road. Great wide-ranging views of Sugar Hill and the swift River Valley can be found at the Sugar Hill Scenic Outlook at 17.6 miles (28 km).

Keep heading west to reach the highest point of the Kancamagus Pass at 21.9 miles (35 km). A stop at the C.L. Graham/Wangan Grounds Scenic Outlook is highly recommended as it has some of the most impressive views of the whole drive. Two rivers have their source here. The Swift River flows east to join the Saco River in Conway before meeting the Atlantic Ocean in Saco, Maine, while the Pemigewasset River flows west before joining the Merrimack River and meeting the Atlantic at Newbury, Massachusetts.

The Loon Area Mountain Ski Resort is at 29 miles (46.5 km), and is the last major site on the route before the Kancamagus Highway reaches its destination in Lincoln.

Above: Multicolored view from Bear Notch Road. It's closed in winter but for the rest of the year it provides access to the Upper Nanamocomuck skiing area and the town of Bartlett.

Far left: The Swift River Lower Falls as the fall foliage starts to change color.

Following pages: Sunset over the Kancamagus Pass.

MUST SEE

The **Albany Covered Bridge** is an iconic picture opportunity. Take time to walk one of the many trails along the route – both the **Boulder Loop Trail** and the short trail to the **Sabbaday Falls** are lovely. You might also choose to make a detour up the winding **Bear Notch Road** to the town of **Bartlett**.

The **Russell-Colbath House**, located between the Jigger Johnson Campground and Oliverian Brook Road, is filled with 19th century period furniture and there is an atmospheric Civil War cemetery close by. Make a stop at the very top of the **Kancamagus Pass**.

MOUNT WASHINGTON AUTO ROAD
NEW HAMPSHIRE

The journey starts at NH-16. At 2017 rates, access to the Mount Washington Auto Road will cost $29 for a car and driver, $9 for adult passengers, and $7 for children aged 5-12. Before getting here check the road is actually open. It is only ever accessible in summer, but the actual opening dates vary from year to year, depending on the weather. Usually, the road is open from mid-May until late October.

FORMERLY KNOWN AS THE MOUNT WASHINGTON CARRIAGE ROUTE, THE MOUNT WASHINGTON AUTO ROAD IS, ASTONISHINGLY, THE USA'S OLDEST MAN-MADE VISITOR ATTRACTION. It first opened in 1861 and has been welcoming tourists every year since. Interestingly, it's not the only way to the summit. A cog railway was constructed in 1869 and it's also possible to hike to the top over a number of trails, including the Crawford Footpath, which is said to be the USA's oldest continually maintained footpath. Construction work on the Auto Road started in 1854. It was a mammoth task. Work could only take place during the summer months and most of the labor was done by hand. Black powder was available to help clear the route but, even then, blasting holes had to be drilled by hand and it gave a modest explosion compared to dynamite, which was invented in 1867. Thousands of tons of rock and stones had to be transported away by horse and cart and the workforce lived in rudimentary shacks that provided scant comfort when the weather turned bad.

Nevertheless, by 1856, the road reached halfway up the mountain. At this time the company behind the project ran out of money and work stopped. The Mount Washington Summit Road Company – which still

Above: Driving the lower section of the Mount Washington Auto Road is a benign experience.

Far left: As higher elevations are reached, the outlooks, and the road itself becomes increasingly dramatic.

MUST SEE

This is a truly unique driving trip – and what you will see depends very much upon the weather. During the ascent up **Mount Washington** (the highest peak in the north east of the USA) travelers drive through four distinct climate zones and, on a clear day, will be rewarded with breath-taking panoramic views.

On days that are less than perfect, this short route is still exciting, offering sights of stunning cloud formations, as well as flurries of snow even in high summer and brutally strong winds. Be prepared for any sort of weather because you can be certain it will be considerably colder at the top than at the bottom!

owns the road – stepped in and completed the road in 1861. A grand opening attended by local dignitaries brought up in a coach was planned for August 8th of that year but, in fact, they were not the first to reach the top. As part of the development of the area, the Glen House Hotel had been opened at the foot of the mountain in 1852 and its owner, a certain Colonel Joseph Thompson, jumped the gun and drove his own horse and carriage to the summit some three weeks before the official opening. His primary aim was not to steal the limelight from the distinguished guests, but to make sure the honor of being the first to the top was not taken by his arch-rival, Colonel John Hitchcock, proprietor of the nearby Alpine House Hotel!

The start of the route takes drivers through the Hardwood climate zone, after which the road climbs through the Canadian and Sub-Alpine zones before reaching the Alpine zone and, finally, the summit at 6,288 feet (1,916 m). The road is not in the best condition so it's important to keep in low gear, driving slowly and carefully. There are numerous steep drop-offs and no guard rails so the driver must also keep his or her eyes on the road and pull in to one of a number of parking areas to enjoy the panoramic views over the Presidential Range. He or she should be prepared for poor weather, too: particularly high winds. Mount Washington sits right in the middle of three weather systems and gusts of up to 100 mph (161 km/h) are not unusual. In 1934, a wind speed of 231 mph (372 km/h) was recorded. If conditions do deteriorate, for safety's sake it is best to turn back and try again another day.

Above: The Cog Railway that takes visitors up Mount Washington. Both steam and diesel trains make the ascent between late April to November.

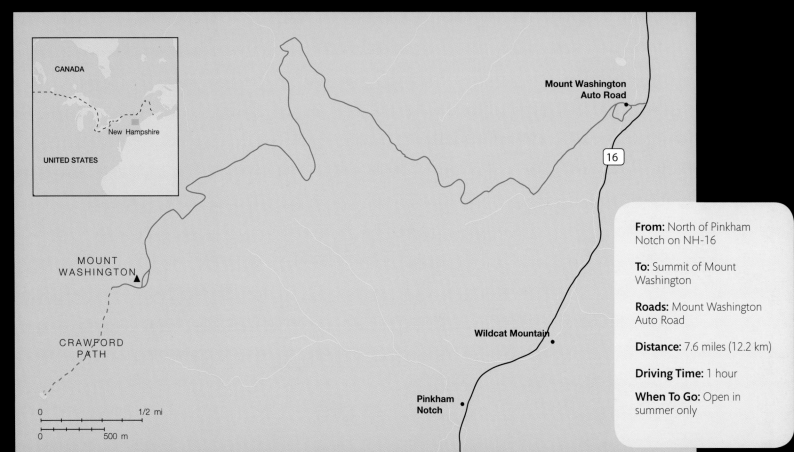

CANADA

New Hampshire

UNITED STATES

Mount Washington
Auto Road

16

MOUNT
WASHINGTON

CRAWFORD
PATH

Wildcat Mountain

Pinkham
Notch

0   1/2 mi

0   500 m

From: North of Pinkham Notch on NH-16

To: Summit of Mount Washington

Roads: Mount Washington Auto Road

Distance: 7.6 miles (12.2 km)

Driving Time: 1 hour

When To Go: Open in summer only

Above: Mount Washington in winter with the Cog Railway clearly visible.

Right: The summit, at 6,288 feet (1,916 m), is the highest in the northeastern United States.

During the ascent, drivers will find that a short section of the road has a gravel surface, where it is even more important to take good care. Don't even think of trying to emulate the professional drivers who compete in the "Climb to the Clouds" event every three years – the record time of 5 minutes, 44 seconds to the top was set in 2017 by Pastrana Travis in a Subaru WRX at a knuckle-whitening average speed of some 96 mph (154 km/h)! Far better to arrive safely, and to hope for clear skies at the summit. Once there, road-trippers will find plenty of parking, and a wooden staircase. By following the final section of the Crawford Path over rocks to the very top of the mountain they will be rewarded with the route's final treasure – incredible views all the way to the Atlantic Ocean.

SEA TO SKY HIGHWAY
BRITISH COLUMBIA

Highway 99 – the Sea-to-Sky Highway – does exactly what its name describes. Journeying from Vancouver at sea level on the Pacific coast of British Columbia, it rises 2,200 feet (670 m) to Whistler in the mountains. Originally a logging trail, and later a very narrow and winding road, it was radically improved and widened in time for the 2010 Olympic Games, a refurbishment that left unchanged the succession of breath-taking ocean, glacier, forest, mountain, and lake views. Unsurprisingly, it is one of BC's most popular driving roads.

THE ROUTE STARTS IN DOWNTOWN VANCOUVER. Head north through Stanley Park and cross Lions Gate Bridge to Horseshoe Bay, which is where the Sea-to-Sky Highway officially begins. That said, many might choose to make a first stop here, visiting Whytecliff Park on the rugged coastline where road-trippers can watch the boats coming into Horseshoe Bay. The lucky might also spot orcas in the cold waters below.

Continue toward Lions Bay, making sure to look out for the fine views over the water to Bowen and Gambier islands. At Mile 9 there's a short walk to Porteau Cove which has great outlooks over Howe Sound.

At around Mile 17 travelers will come to Britannia Beach on the site of the former Britannia Copper Mine. The old mine ceased operations in 1970 but is now a fascinating museum where visitors can descend

Above: The Sea to Sky Highway between Squamish and Whistler. The road was upgraded in time for the 2010 Winter Olympics.

Right: The Sky Pilot Suspension Bridge that runs between the Spirit Trail and the Spirit Viewing Platform at the top of the Sea to Sky Gondola offers amazing views for those with a head for heights.

into some of the 130 miles (210 km) of tunnels some 2,000 feet (600 m) underground. A little north of Britannia, Shannon Falls is another of the many spectacular waterfalls along the way. Travelers who cannot manage more difficult hiking will want to stop here. A very easy walking trail from the road allows visitors to get up close to the misty base of the towering waterfall.

Left: Lions Gate Bridge connects the City of Vancouver to the North Shore municipalities of the District of North Vancouver.

Below right: The Brandywine waterfall in Brandywine Falls Provincial Park tumbles 230 foot (70 m) down the hillside.

Following pages: Garibaldi Lake near Whistler is one of the most popular hiking destinations in British Columbia with some 56 miles (90 km) of trails open year round.

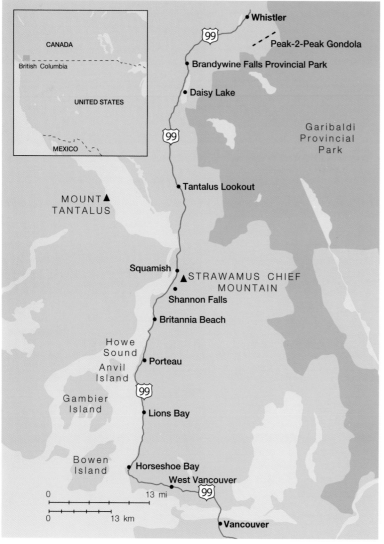

From: Vancouver

To: Whistler

Roads: Highway 99

Distance: 85 miles (137 km)

Driving Time: 2.5 hours

When To Go: Best in spring summer and fall

MUST SEE

This dramatic highway can be driven in a little over two hours but many take a couple of days over the journey simply because there are so many dramatic sights and so much to experience along the route.

Whytecliff Park has fabulous ocean views, and the **Britannia Mine Museum**, **Shannon Falls**, and the **Sea-to-Sky Gondola** at Squamish are also well worth a visit.

Further along the route, take in **Tantalus Lookout**, **Garibaldi Provincial Park**, and **Brandywine Falls** before arriving in **Whistler**.

Continue north and, just before reaching Squamish, Stawamus Chief Mountain comes into view. This dramatic and almost sheer cliff is a major attraction for climbers. For hikers, there is a six mile (9.5 km) trail that leads up to the top where there are panoramic views of the waters below and the snow-covered mountains to the north. For everyone else, there is the Sea-to-Sky Gondola, which opened in 2014 and allows access for all, including those in wheelchairs. The 10-minute sky ride brings visitors to Summit Lodge and amazing 360 degree views. At the very top tourists can also cross the vertiginous Sky Pilot Suspension Bridge that runs between the Spirit Trail and the Spirit Viewing Platform.

Squamish itself is a buzzy town set at the top of the 26-mile (42 km) long Howe Sound. Founded as a logging town, it is now a vibrant hub for climbers, mountain bikers, sailors, and kite-boarders. It also has a number of excellent, locally-owned, restaurants and bars, which make this a good place for a stop.

Keep heading north up Highway 99 and consider a stop at Tantalus Lookout, at 1,050 feet (320 m) elevation. From here there are great views of the Tantalus Mountain range. As with so many places along this route, there are also a number of easy hiking trails that allow visitors to fully explore the beauty and variety of British Colombia's unspoilt habitats.

For those with plenty of time on their hands, the Garibaldi Provincial Park is a must, too. Named for the 8,786 foot (2,678 m) Mount Garibaldi, visitors here will find rich geological history, beautiful lakes, snow-topped mountains, and an abundance of wildlife including deer, bears, and eagles. Some 56 miles (90 km) of hiking trails are open year-round.

A little further toward Whistler is the Brandywine Falls Provincial Park where the major feature is the 230 foot (70 m) Brandywine waterfall, though it is worth lingering for the tranquil scenes provided by Daisy Lake with its mountainous backdrop.

The route finishes in Whistler, one of the world's great ski resorts. Unlike many other such towns, this is very much a year-round community. Outside the ski season it offers hiking, biking, bear viewing, golf, white water rafting, jet boating, and any number of other outdoor activities. The end of the route offers one, last special opportunity: the second gondola ride along the Sea-to-Sky Highway. The peak-2-Peak Gondola in Whistler modestly describes itself as "Not your average gondola ride". This is a massive understatement. In fact, it is the longest and highest lift in the world. At 2.71 miles (4.4 km) long, it runs some 1,427 feet (436 m) above the valley floor between Whistler and the Blackcomb Mountains. Summer or winter, it's an astonishing experience.

CABOT TRAIL
NOVA SCOTIA

The Cabot Trail – one of the world's most picturesque circular road trails – takes in much of Nova Scotia's Cape Breton Island with the dramatic Atlantic Ocean to the east and north and the Gulf of St. Lawrence to the west. It's named after the famous Italian navigator Giovanni Caboto, better known as John Cabot, the man who landed here in 1497 after crossing the Atlantic on an expedition funded by King Henry VIII of England.

IN TOTAL, IT'S 185 MILES (297 KM) IN LENGTH AND CAN BE COMPLETED IN AROUND FIVE HOURS OR SO. However, there are two points to consider. First is that once you have started, you have to complete the trail as there are no short cuts you can take. Second is that the vistas are so dramatic and there is so much to see and do that most people take two or three days or even longer to complete the journey – especially if you choose to take on some of the famous hiking trails in the Cape Breton Highlands National Park such as Le Vieux Chemin du Cap-Rouge up Jerome Mountain starting at Trout Brook or the Sunset Hike on the Skyline Trail which finishes 1,300 feet (400 m) above the ocean where hopefully you will see pilot and minke whales as the sun drops below the horizon.

Right: The sinuous Cabot Trail that follows the coast of Nova Scotia is one of the most spectacular roads in the world. This is where it passes through the Cape Breton Highlands National Park.

MUST SEE

This is a journey of magnificent sea views, wonderful highland scenery, and spectacular wildlife – including whales, bald eagles, and moose.

There is also something along the trail for every taste and interest – such as a whiskey tour of the **Glencora Distillery**, a visit to the **Alexander Bell National Historic Site**, boat trips for **whale-watching** up-close, a golf course at **Ingonish** voted one of the finest in Canada, fly-fishing at **Margaree Harbor**, and some of the finest hiking trails in **Nova Scotia**.

Above: Exterior of the Alexander Graham Bell National Historic Site in the town of Baddeck at the start of the Cabot Trail.

Far right: Follow the Cabot Trail in the fall and see it resplendent in magnificently colored foliage.

Following pages: The spectacular Bras d'Or Lake at Baddeck Harbor with its lighthouse.

The trail can be tackled in either direction but we will take it counter clockwise. Starting in Baddeck, check out the Alexander Graham Bell National Historic Site and learn about the invention of the telephone before joining the Nova Scotia Highway 105 at Exit 7 and continue toward St. Ann's Bay until Exit 11 and take a left turn onto Trunk 30, clearly marked the Cabot Trail.

You are now on the famous Cabot Trail, a highway opened in 1932 to connect otherwise isolated fishing villages around the Cape Breton coast. It's a stunning piece of engineering as for much of the trail the road has been carved out of rugged highlands, perched precariously over the ocean. There are numerous sharp and blind bends, some vertiginous drops, and steep climbs and ascents. What this means is that you would be well advised to make sure your car is well serviced (and has brakes and tires in good order), and take your time to enjoy the views.

After passing a number of small villages, enter the Cape Breton Highlands National Park where you will need cash to pay an entrance fee and collect a map showing all the trails and sites of interest within the park. Next you will reach Ingonish where the Middle Head Trail for hikers and the Highland Links for golfers provide possible stopovers.

The main trail now heads inland for South Harbor but you can take a coastal deviation via Neil's Harbor before regaining the main Cabot Trail. Carry on across the northeast tip of Cape Breton to Pleasant Bay on the Gulf of St. Lawrence, a great place for whale watching where you can also visit the Whale Interpretive Centre to learn about these ocean leviathans.

To see whales close up, stop in Chéticamp where a number of the whale-watching cruise companies guarantee a sighting or return your money. You are also likely to see moose on the hills and bald eagles in the skies.

Continue along the trail to Margaree Harbor where you can do a spot of fly-fishing, visit the Salmon Museum or indulge in various watersports. The remainder of the trail crosses green verdant farmland as it follows the Margaree River Valley back toward Baddeck and journey's end.

From: Baddeck, Cape Breton Island

To: Baddeck, Cape Breton Island

Roads: Trunk 30, and Nova Scotia Highway 105 from Exit 7-11

Distance: 185 miles (297 km)

Driving Time: 5 hours minimum

When To Go: Year-round but best in spring, summer, and fall.

PICTURE CREDITS